FOOD

PRESENTATION & DISPLAY

FOOD
PRESENTATION & DISPLAY

Edited by Martin M. Pegler

Retail Reporting Corporation, New York

Retail Reporting Corporation
101 Fifth Avenue
New York, NY 10003

Distributors to the trade in the United States and Canada
Van Nostrand Reinhold
115 Fifth Avenue
New York, NY 10003

Distributed outside of the United States and Canada
Hearst Books International
105 Madison Avenue
New York, NY 10016

Library of Congress Cataloging in Publication Data:
Main Entry under the title: Food Presentation & Display

Printed and Bound in Hong Kong
ISBN 0-934590-41-9

Designed by Judy Shepard

TABLE OF CONTENTS

INTRODUCTION

What is the difference between a cafe — a cafeteria — a grill — a diner? The answer is not in this book because it is no more than a name and as Juliet and many other diners might ask: "What's in a name? That which we call a diner, by any other name would prepare food as fresh and tasty." Is the food less fair — less well prepared or presented? Is the ambience less alive — less fun and filled with theater and spectacle? Cafes have delis and delis often feature cafes. Diners sell take-out food and take-out food shops invite those who want to sit down and dine. Markets have restaurants attached and even restaurants may feature a market where diners who just can't have enough of a good thing can take some home with them. What succeeds today is not necessarily specialization as giving the customers what they want — where they want it and in a manner that complements their lifestyle or social status. Customers want comfort, conveniences, clean, well-lit spaces, a degree of ambience — and a banquet for their senses. They want to see what they buy and they want to see it well displayed, coordinated and accessorized — under flattering lights just as though it were an outfit to be worn for dining out. For years we have been educating consumers to accept only the best — because they are worth it so why should they accept less than the best when it comes to food?

Food is more than a source of substenance. If we ate food only to stay alive and function we could probably exist on all sorts of bottled glucose liquids of assorted colors, vitamin pills and "supplements" — but would that be "living"? Food and dining have always been a part of social status and I'm sure who got the least burnt part of animal must have counted for favor even with the cavemen. The food we ate — where it came from and how it was prepared and where we ate our meal have always been facets of who we are and where we belong and on what rung of the social ladder we are poised. Today people dine where they can be seen dining and the long popular European concept of street-side dining is becoming very popular in certain areas of the country — and with certain people; they want to watch but also be watched.

Diners don't want too many surprises and with food preparation becoming more international in scope — more universal in menu choices with exotic and sometimes unpronounceable names — it is reassuring to see what the dish looks like — and what went into it before it appears camouflaged under a sauce or topping or floriated garnish. Thus, open kitchens are again becoming the focal points of design in restaurants. As of old when you could order a hamburger and watch it being grilled — or see a sandwich layered before your eyes — not removed prepacked or preboxed from a heated chute — you are part of the preparation, and the preparation is part of the enjoyment of the food. Whether it is watching a pizza round being pounded, kneaded and tossed — or sushi and sushimi being skinned, sliced or wrapped — or vegetables being wokked back and forth — or tortillas being patted between palms — it is all entertainment. And, when the ambience takes on the trappings of a stage set and gets into the act with the "performers" the diners feel that they are part of an unfolding spectacle and that the food that arrives is worth whatever the bill is that follows after. It was fun, the food "tasted" better and the diners participated in the creation of the repast — just as they do when they "create" their own salads from the expanse of vegetables, condiments and complementary toppings — or when they make their critical decisions at a groaning buffet table.

This book speaks to the issue of food as spectacle — a delight to the eye — as entertainment for all our senses — as theater where we mortals may dine upon what our eyes have relished — and relish what we shop for and what we eat in stimulating surroundings. It is a book that salutes the store designer, the lighting, the fixturing, the visual merchandising and the displays that make mere morsels of sustenance into sublime tidbits that soothe the soul, stir the senses and activates the salivary glands.

Bon Appetit.

Martin M. Pegler, S.V.M.

FOOD

PRESENTATION & DISPLAY

GOURMET-TO-GO

We run to the future only to return to the past. None of us are truly old enough to remember the old general store that grew-up and developed in the little town on the prairie. We probably do have visions of what that store looked like but they are based on either re-creations in historical settings — or things we saw in the western movies of the '50s and '60s. For me the old general store is a place of sights, smells and textures — of cracker barrels open for tasting and taking — coarse brown burlap sacks filled with coffee beans, red beans, nuts, rice and potatoes — wooden bushels and baskets brimming over with red apples and other seasonal fruits — heavy pressed glass jars filled with jaw-breakers, jelly beans and penny candy (what's a penny?). There are wooden shelves lined up with colorful boxes and tins wearing labels and logos that are now collector's items and someplace an old, rustic hutch or cupboard plays host to jars of homemade jams, jellies and preserves in mason jars capped with bright bits of gingham and calico. Freshly baked breads and muffins are displayed on flat straw baskets snuggled up in checkered, homespun napkins. Cider in wooden kegs is joined by milk and cream in galvanized containers and the copper kettle is up and steaming on the wood burning stove in the middle of the shop — for anyone who wants to stop for a mug of tea. Sounds familiar — doesn't it? This 19th century food and clothing emporium is a forerunner of today's mall and food court. Things really haven't changed that much except for the neon and chrome as we graduated from general stores to more food-oriented grocery stores only to seek solutions in more and more non-specializing supermarkets than to return to the warmth, charm and friendliness of food once again on display in textured surroundings, under low-keyed lights in areas where people stop to taste — to shop — to meet and to sit awhile.

Instead of simple treats today our more sophisticated — and internationalized tastes seek out the specialty foods prepared by chefs from gourmet recipes often with exotic and imported ingredients. Also, we want to eat our cake and have it too; to take home or to the office but to sample it before we go. This chapter, Gourmet-To-Go contains a collection of grown-up grocery stores that have gone gourmet — markets with up-scaled and sophisticated attitudes and products — delis with and without delusions of grandeur — and food areas in department stores where specialty foods and products are available prepared, prepackaged or put up to-go. Most of our examples have managed to move a few crates and cartons aside and make room for the patron who wants to sample the wares or indulge in a quick break or snack. The tables and chairs become "the cafe" and the grocery or market enters into the nineties with customer comfort and convenience as an integral part of the store's layout and design.

Sutton Place Gourmet
Alexandria, VA

SUTTON PLACE GOURMET

Alexandria, VA

The concept of this upscaled "department store for food" is "to provide the finest quality food products available including rare and unusual items, combined with the considerate service of a knowledgable staff." Sutton Place Gourmet was started ten years ago and now has three handsome locations in the Washington area. The interior of this, the largest and newest of the chain, is an inviting and pleasant blend of mauve tones accented with deep dark green plus the sparkle of brass. Friendly wood faced fixtures are set out under the excellent lighting to delight the shoppers. Among the sixteen individual "departments" that are laid out in a leisurely traffic plan for the shoppers to peruse is the bakery where baking "from scratch" fills the air with the fragrance of just-baked foods. There is also a deli, a prepared foods area supervised by master chef Bank Szerenyi, an international cheese bazaar, an unending selection of coffees and teas beautifully displayed in brass and glass cannisters, and rows and rows of carefully arranged groceries and delicacies imported from everywhere. Great attention is given to the visual merchandising of the foods in the illuminated showcases and on floor stands. Mark Berey, president and C.E.O. of the company says, "that is part of the statement of who we are and what we are about. The quality product we're producing deserves a quality presentation." The company was founded with the intention of being a full service department store style gourmet food emporium and its credo is their slogan: "The extraordinary everyday food market."

PERELANDRA'S

Brooklyn Heights, NY

Perelandra's is an organic food store/deli located in the re-emerging area of Brooklyn which is becoming home for up-scaled New Yorkers who have crossed over the bridge looking for something different. The architects selected an open plan design concept to do justice to the variety of products being offered and also to create the desired ambience that would encourage health-aware shoppers to browse at ease. The careful planning, the use of display shelves made of natural red oak combined with ceramic tiles and the warm friendly atmosphere makes shopping a voyage of discovery with easy access to the deli and food preparation areas. The warm woody interior, even the floor is wood, is well illuminated by incandescent drop lights from the gridded ceiling. Perelandra's has the feeling of the old fashioned corner grocery store updated with style and sophistication to suit the smart new shoppers.

Arch.: SRK Architects, Philadelphia, PA
Assoc. in charge/Design principal: Ron Pompei
Architect of record: S. Neil Schlosser
Photographer: Matt Wargo

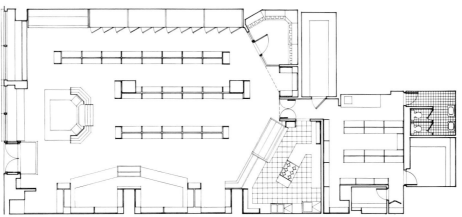

QUADRANT

Chicago, IL

This shop is a prototype design for a "mini-mall" of 3000 to 4000 square feet to fit into a typical shopping mall space. The complementary product areas are differentiated by different visual "sets." The candy/sales area is designed to directly complement the Espresso bar opposite. The designers/architects state, "If the traditional espresso bar is conceived of as the 'old made new,' the candy/cards area is to be the 'new made old.'" Although patterns, forms and structures are contemporary, the materials and wall treatments suggest that they have been aged; "a vision of a future already past." A variety of metals are rusted and the walls are weathered in a complex mixture of textured paints. Shelving is hung away from the walls and backlit. A cabinet sheathed in "steel armor" encloses the sales computer and also provides an elevated display surface. Natural woods are used on some of the floor fixtures and the floor is finished in a striking black and white checkered pattern. The ceiling is painted out with a deep full green and the targeted lights warm up the merchandise offerings.

Design: Florian-Wierzbowski, Chicago, IL
Graphic Design: Rick Valicenti, Thirst
Mural Artist: V.A. Pintor
Photographs: Bernadette Planert, Florian/Wierzbowski
Don Dubroff, Sadin Photographers

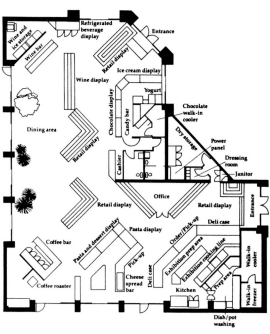

PANACHE

Fullerton, CA

For this combination restaurant/grocery/delicatessen/wine shop/ice cream parlor, the owners selected to build their 6500 sq. ft. emporium in the well-to-do but conservative community of Fullerton. The shop is housed in an old red brick building and the interior is filled with light and color and seems to be endless in space mainly due to the white walls, the checkered floors, and the neon signs and graphics that delineate the product areas — all in bright pastels — and all under a sky painted ceiling. Around part of the store floor-to-ceiling brick arched windows allow the daylight to flood onto the floor and onto the white canvas umbrellas that "shelter" the tables in the dining area; reinforcing the indoor-outdoor theme of Panache. Panache is French for "flamboyant in style or action" and it aptly describes Deborah DuShanes approach to putting together this cluster of

gourmet shops under one roof. There are fourteen separate departments in this burgeoning layout that includes in addition to the restaurant that can accommodate 100 persons, a coffee bar, wine bar, chocolate shop, bakery gourmet shop with specialties from all over the world and a gourmet-to-go deli.

Michael Bolton, the architect/designer used lights to add to the retail impact with downlights over the refrigeration equipment and the fixed shelves, the track mounted lights to highlight the changing displays. The low energy neon adds sparkle and glitz and the incandescents illuminate where the customers congregate. Panache is laid out on the diagonal since the space is an odd-shaped L in plan. With this technique "you can't turn around without being sold something visually, you get both a distant focus and a point of sales focus."

Architect/Design: Bolton Design Group, Carmel Valley, CA

BAREFOOT CONTESSA

East Hampton, NY

Out in the Hamptons where living is easy and the "casual" is a way of life is this charmingly casual food shop which combines gourmet-style prepared food to go as well as the "makings" for those who would rather do it themselves. Provincial styled cupboards and dressers of scrubbed pine serve as display cases and as the checkout counters up front where freshly baked muffins and cakes fight for display space with other colorful and tempting last minute purchases. Up front freshly ground coffees and teas intermingle their scents with fresh flowers. Everything is on display and display is everything. According to Ina Garten, the owner, "placing foods on counters so that people can see what they will be eating is what sells." Immediately upon entering the shopper is treated to a beautiful and bountiful array of exotic fruits, fresh vegetables and local produce stuffed into and overflowing from baskets, bushels and wood boxes. Farther back in the shop are smoked fish, charcuterie, cheeses and the prepared foods designed to appeal to the developed tastes of the patrons of the Barefoot Contessa. In addition to gourmet-to-go salads and main dishes — the Contessa also caters parties large and small.

Designer/owner: Ina Garten

FOOD FESTIVAL

New York, NY

The client for this gourmet grocery wanted an "Italian market" look; openly displayed fresh foods. The client also wanted a quality designed space that would appeal to the affluent community around the newly constructed office building that would house the 3500 sq. ft. Food Festival on its ground floor. Today the shopper here can find wet and dry vegetables, organic produce, flowers, freshly baked breads, deli items, a salad bar, bulk nuts, grain, tea and coffee and a coffee roaster.

The displayer fixtures are placed on angles to avoid the usual long aisles associated with grocery stores. Within the structure of the design the designers provided a modular system of assorted size boxes and baskets which can be used throughout the store in ever changing configurations. A yellow sunburst covers the lowest point of the ducting system in the ceiling and it serves as a decorative focal point. A custom oak grid covers the remaining ceiling with the structural and mechanical elements behind the grid painted blue. Lighting is simple and an assortment of PAR lamps are used on the adaptable track system — fitting the lamp to the item being lit.

Design: Evelyn Sherwood Designs, Inc., NY
Photographer: John Ferrentino, Harrington Pk., NJ

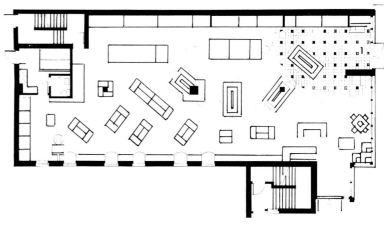

GREENWICH MARKET

New York, NY

According to the designer, Tony Chi, "the entire concept is based on the idea of not having a separate storage room." So, boxes are stacked right out on the mini-tiled floor, and movable ladders swing around the fascia providing access to the shelves under the 13' high ceiling. "The labels and the bright colors of the packaging materials provide the lively backdrop for the small cafe up front."

This is a "new old-style deli" that was created to appeal to the people who live and work on this southern tip of Manhattan Island. The store is painted white and it is brightly accented with red metal trim and red ladders. Natural wood adds the familiar warmth associated with wood and the space is filled with light streaming down from the track lights on the ceiling and from the fluted glass drop lights over the well displayed counters. Burlap bags and woven baskets line up on the floor — nudging the cartons of stock — and overflow with fruits, nuts and breads. The old fashioned glass jars on the marble counter are filled with colorful candies and treats. The dropped ceiling behind the counter is surfaced with panels of patterned metal painted white. It is an inviting shop; it invites you in for a cup of coffee and you stay long enough to buy food for a party.

Design: Tony Chi/Albert Chen and Assoc., NY
Photographer: Max Andrews

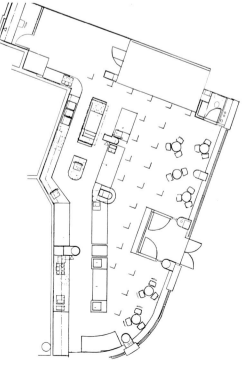

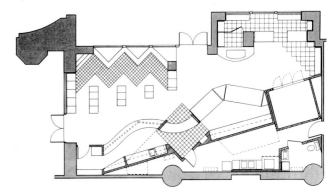

COMPLEMENTS

Rincon Center, San Francisco, CA

Complements is a most unique gourmet-to-go shop that features a range of imported packaged delicacies, a large wine selection as well as a coffee/espresso bar along with bins filled with assorted exotic blends of coffee to buy. In the refrigerator cases there is an endless variety of cheeses and prepared meats and the dessert offerings are temptingly arranged behind glass shields — at eye level.

Most of the floor and stock fixtures are made of natural wood and they are flattered by the rose tinted concrete floors, the expansive areas of sculptured cool blue walls, and the deep dubonnet laminated counters. The stand-up refrigerator becomes a focal point encased in black tiles up to the black painted ceiling. Some of the walls have been mottled and "textured" with the other colors in the shop's palette. Air ducts are used as decorative elements and the perimeter walls are notched, keyholed, recessed and sculpted with architectural shapes and forms. Can-like adjustable light fixtures hang down and provide light on the merchandise while other lights from the dropped ceiling over the counters and the coffee bar illuminate these areas.

Design: Levy Design Partners, San Francisco, CA
Prin. Arch. in Charge: Toby S. Levy
Decorative Painted Finish: Peggy Del Rosario

IRVINE RANCH FARMER'S MARKET

Horton Plaza, San Diego, CA

In the lower level of the visually stimulating Horton Plaza can be found this wonderland of fresh fruits, vegetables, salads and salad bars. There is a delicatessen and a bakery and anything to quench the thirst or satisfy the hunger of a shopper in the mall or a health minded secretary or executive from the many office buildings surrounding the market and its open to the sun outdoor dining tables.

With all the brilliant colors of the produce and the packaging to make the impact the setting is neutral; mostly white and black

with welcoming touches of dark green. The walls, floors and fascias are all finished in white accented with black. Easy to read signage in black or white appears above eye level and the black and white checkerboard pattern is used on the floors and behind the service areas on the white tiled walls. The charcoal gridded ceiling that covers most of the market is pierced with fluorescent fixtures and supports the ridged pressed glass drop-lights that supply the incandescent light where it is needed. More fluorescents are used over and behind the service counters.

Design: Beckham & Eisenman, Irvine, CA
Photographer: Milroy/McAleer, Newport Beach, CA

1st CANADIAN PLACE FOOD MARKET

Toronto, Ont., Canada

Located in an office/retail complex, the designers were faced with the challenge of upgrading an existing market in keeping with the new identity and image projected by the office tower. The changes were affected by using solid Honduras mahogany woodworking teamed with upscaled materials like sandblasted glass, marble and brass accents. The original quarry tile was replaced by a handsome floor patterned with peach, gray and green granites. A warm pleasant peach color was used on the ceiling and coupled with the uplights it tended to expand the sense of spaciousness. Quartz downlights now highlight the main circulation patterns. Mahogany and marble "demising caps" separate and accentuate each tenants' facade as well as delineate each space. The store fronts have been unified by continuous suspended moldings. Special lighting fixtures were designed in antique brass and opal glass to reinforce the traditional detailing of the area and a custom clock, which is visible from the main traffic areas, symbolically is reminiscent of old fashioned marketplaces.

Design: Camdi International, Montreal, Que.
Project Manager: Patty Xenos

BALDUCCI'S

New York, NY

Balducci's is a "landmark" establishment for food in old Greenwich Village. The 6000 sq. ft. space is crammed with cases overspilling with meats, cheeses, dipped chocolates, outrageous desserts, tempting breadstuffs, seafood and fish — even a lobster tank, fresh pastas of every description, gourmet coffee beans and so much more. As the shopper wanders through the cramped and crowded aisles sharing space with the provolones, salamis, hams in snoods and braided sausages swinging overhead along with myriad baskets he/she steps gingerly around build-ups of cans of imported olive oil and baskets and crates brimming with dewy fresh produce. It takes restraint not to want to taste everything. The dimly, but effectively, lit store exudes "old world charm" — it looks, smells and feels the way an Italian grocery is supposed to. You expect to find an old

Italian grandmother, basket on arm, shopping around the next display.

Displays are of paramount concern and the fresh fruits and vegetables that arrive daily from all over the world are artfully arranged into eye-arresting compositions and challenge the equally well thought out and designed display of whole and cut wheels of Parmigiano Reggi and Balducci's own forcacia. Balducci makes its own fresh and smoked mozzarella which is rushed three times daily to the store. In addition there is a sinful presentation, in the center of the shop, of beautifully prepared and decorated foods ready to travel.

The shopper is literally bombarded by the smells and sights in this atmospheric, cramped, crowded but delightfully comfortable market.

THE VERMONT COUNTRY KITCHEN

Middlebury, VT

The Vermont Country Kitchen is an attractive combination of 18th century Vermont charm tied on to a twentieth century European cafe. The setting is a remodeled 1799 residence set on a knoll in the center of town and painted a sunny yellow. The original house contains the specialty foods and wine shop and there is a work area on the second level for the extensive gift basket business. This shop is filled with small areas and corners, — each corner devoted to a different aspect of the shop's stock; Vermont products, chocolates, wines, coffees, gifts. A turn-of-the-century cast iron, wood burning stove in the center of the shop is used to display cookwear. Other unusual display and stock fixtures are an old Vermont wagon seat, Adirondack twig tables, a Country-French hutch, old apple boxes and antique oak tables set out on braided rugs almost as old.

In contrast, the addition which houses the cafe is a former garage. It is stark white with quarry tile floors and the contemporary look comes from the cobalt and white tiles used above the counters. A high oval window, two skylights and an atrium door keep the area flooded with daylight all year round. The kitchen and preparation areas are open with large flour bins and stock pots stacked to separate the seating area from the kitchen. "One of the greatest assets we have in the shop is the wonderful smells of soups and baked goods being prepared," says Cathy Nief, the owner. "The olefactory and the visual create a wonderful sense of home."

Design: Cathy Nief, Owner

PASTA AND CHEESE

Santa Monica, CA

On Montana Avenue, a street rapidly upscaling and blossoming forth with designer shops and smart retail stores, this tiny corner shop takes on all corners. The owner/designer has made this shop a personal statement and it is warm, friendly and inviting. The prepared foods and pastas are attractively presented in the brick and wood trimmed interior which is mostly white. Straw baskets float overhead and on the floor more baskets hold French and Italian breads. On the counter, baskets beckon with baked goods. A track light suspended from the high ceiling brings the warming light down closer to the products displayed on top of the cases. Two tiny white cafe tables with matching chairs can seat the fortunate few who step in for some fresh coffee or a quick pasta fix. It also serves as Jim Deely's office when talking to clients about the parties he caters.

Designer/Owner: Jim Deely

FOODSTUFFS

Chicago, IL

This is a prototype design for a foremost purveyor of prepared foods in the midwest. According to the designers, "white floors, plants and metal surfaces express an emphasis on cleanliness and freshness to the customer. Displays which include antique furniture emphasize the traditional lifestyle values and high quality." A central island for coffee, cheese and specialty prepared foods is distinguished by a canopy of trusswork supported by four columns which enclose the refrigerator cases. This island, seen right, dominates the 2500 sq. ft. sales area. Along the perimeter wall high tech, commercial shelving units hold the packaged gourmet foods and wines. A pastry kitchen, fresh seafood and meat area is visible from the street. Checkout and catering are combined with impulse items such as bread and flowers up in the front window.

Design/architecture: Florian/Wierzbowski, Chicago, IL
Photographer: Mark Ballogg, Steinkamp/Ballogg

37

BLOOMINGDALES

Chicago, IL

In the Marketplace the fine woodworking and the Frank Lloyd Wright inspirations that make the rest of the store so elegant and distinguished is continued for the housing and presentation of prepared and packaged foods and sweets. Specially designed counters of light woods accented with black are complemented by refrigerator cases with wood veneered facings. Overhead the ceiling is patterned with fluorescent fixtures and recessed and exposed incandescent lamps. Beneath the wood trimmed fascias on the perimeter walls fluorescent tubes light up the packaged products. The floor is finished with white and mauve/gray ceramic tiles. The refinement and elegance of the color scheme and detailing is also reflected in the Espresso Bar which is part of the Marketplace.

Design: Hambrecht Terrell International, NY

SPIESS

Randhurst S/C, Mt. Prospect, IL

Readily available commercial metal shelving units are finished in white and divided up by occasional provincial styled natural pine cupboards and cabinets. The area is marked off with a checkerboard border of gray and white ceramic tiles which in turn is outlined with dark gray marble. The area is all white from the white tiled floor to the tables and chairs and the white enameled pipes that support the floating lamps that light up the counter. The white perimeter wall is decorated with a border of gray and white tiles. The dropped ceiling is filled with fluorescent fixtures but there are many incandescent pendant lamps dangling from the arced rods to warm up the product presentations.

Design: Schafer Associates, Oakbrook Terrace, IL

KA DE WE

The famous food floor opened in 1956 and has become a legend. This "rendezvous for Gourmets" is on the sixth floor and can be reached by a non-stop express elevator. It is the largest food department in Europe (5,100 sq. meters) and the second largest in the world. The shopper can find 25,000 edible items here including 400 kinds of bread and 1800 types of cheese. Each week 20,000 tons of fruit, vegetables, meat, fish and cheese are purchased and three times each week fresh fish is flown in in refrigerated containers from France, Israel, Turkey and German seaports. Fruits and vegetables also come from all over the world. The most renowned French gourmet houses and master chefs have branches on the sixth floor of KaDeWe. "The choice ranges from Lenotre to Fauchon and Bocuse, but also extends as far as stalls of beer and bouilettes."

A newly redesigned Fresh Fish area has taken its place on Six and it sparkles with glass, gray marbled walls, and slick black cases — all highlighted and accented with gleaming brass tubing. The area is brilliant with light from rows of incandescents lined up on the ceiling. The snack area and bar are extensions of this newly renovated area with the light gray marble floor inset with black diamond designs.

Design: Norbert Konnecke

THE FOOD HALL AT STRAWBRIDGE & CLOTHIER

Philadelphia, P.A

In a venerable store filled with venerable traditions, the Food Hall at Strawbridge & Clothier is somewhat reminiscent of Harrod's but on a smaller scale. The building's traditional architecture — the 20' high ceilings, the panels and moldings, the patterned marble floors, the rich dark woodworking — all add to the special character of this food shop. The floor fixtures are mainly of dark mahogany highlighted with brass detailing and the candy area has the look and feel of the century gone by. The ribbed, pressed glass pendant lighting fixtures add to the nostalgic atmosphere while they provide a warm glow on the displays on the solid looking tables below.

Two long runs of refrigerated cases make up the major food presentation statement in the Hall. Dark green is the accent color here and green tiles sheath some of the columns enclosed between the self illuminated cases that display cheese, meats, salads and prepared food-to-go. An elaborate and decorative "crown" of drop lights with green metal lamp shades hangs over the cases and add extra warmth to the merchandise below. The same green color is used on the logo that appears everywhere, on graphics and on wrappings and bags.

The tea and coffee area could be a free standing shop on its own. The same traditional "good-old-days" look takes over in the dining area which is filled with dark woods, brass, crystal drop lights and the menu written on a mahogany framed blackboard.

Visual Merchandising Director: Jon Witmeyer

MARSHALL FIELDS, "DOWN UNDER"

Chicago, IL

One of the first areas of renovation of the Marshall Fields flagship store was the Down Under space on the lower level. In addition to a variety of gourmet food counters and packaged foods shelved areas several fast food shops were included in the new food area along with an elegant cafe for snacking or lunching. One stand, shown here, carries neon graphics as the signage on the low fascia that runs around the whole space, and the faceted front is faced with brown and white ceramic tiles decorated with patterned tile inserts. The floor is white tile highlighted with a black border and black and white laminates sheath the supporting columns that also act as dividers between the food stands.

The Cafe is sleek and elegant and also done in black and white. The Bauhaus influence can be seen here. The counter and rear splash wall are veneered with small ceramic tiles in a grid pattern and black tiles are set into the white rear wall under the black and stainless steel bands that define the Cafe. In addition to the recessed lamps in the ceiling, bright lights hang down over the counter on long black rods. The floor, here, is also covered with a grid of small white tiles relieved with black.

Design: Hambrecht Terrell International, NY

MARSHALL FIELDS

Water Tower, Chicago, IL

In remodeling this 15-year-old, multi-level store, special attention was given to the Gourmet food area and the Cafe. The floor carries the strong decorative motif; a bold geometric pattern executed in brown, black and white — the three colors that make up the color scheme of the space. In this view the prepared foods are visible in the wood faced glass showcases as well as on shelves and in the wood "bookcases" that add a traditional and "residential" quality to the shop. From the floor up to the pendant light track all is traditional and homey — even the displays on the shelf that runs across the creamy fascia. The tungsten halogen lamps held on the suspended black rods are ultra contemporary and they add sparkling light to the displays and to the prepared foods below. The dining area, beyond, is crisply executed in black and white with contemporary styled furniture and dark gray glass panels.

Design: Walker Group/CNI, NY

PROFFITTS

Biltmore Sq. Mall, Asheville, NC

The Gourmet Food and Gift Shop is part of the Home Store and it appears as an island within the area just off the main aisle. Peach/pink and cool blue are used to enliven the otherwise white scheme. The counters and most of the floor fixtures and cubes are white laminate trimmed with natural oak. A pair of provincial pine tables follow the angle of the border on the floor and bring forward a display of some of the packaged gifts to meet the shoppers on the aisle. The merchandise is presented on several levels — starting on the floor and building up to eye level. The major construction behind the surrounding cases and counters is divided into bays of shelving to show off more packaged merchandise to all the four aisles around the shop. It is painted a rich peach/pink and accented with the blue and white. Signage and displays are applied to the fascia. In addition to the baffled fluorescents in the ceiling, the all important partition is illuminated by long tracks of spots on either side. Brass dish drop lights hang over the chocolate showcase that faces the main aisle.

Design: Schafer Associates, Oakbrook Terrace, IL
Photographer: Jamie Padgett, Karant & Assoc., Chicago, IL

BELK HANES

Winston Salem, NC

The black and white checkerboard floor makes the main design
statement in the Food Area of this department store. The pattern is also raised up and used to band the columns, to outline
the ceiling and to accentuate the arced cabinet that holds the
selection of wines. It is even used to frame the signage on the
perimeter wall. The area is painted white and the counters are
finished with white laminates. Oak wood is used to outline the
wine cabinet, to edge the shelves and to border the tables in the
restaurant area. Oak tables are employed as display elevations
off the main aisle. Fluorescents, hidden behind the wood banded fascia that also serves as a display shelf, light up the ceiling.
Track lights with cannister containers illuminate the cased merchandise and the displays on the tables. To provide a happy
brightness to the dining area, brass pendant lamps are added to
the lighting plan.

Displays are in evidence throughout the area; on feature tables,
on shelves, counters, in baskets on the floor and in baskets under
the ceiling.

Design: Schafer Associates, Oakbrook Terrace, IL
Photographer: Jamie Padgett, Karant & Assoc., Chicago, IL

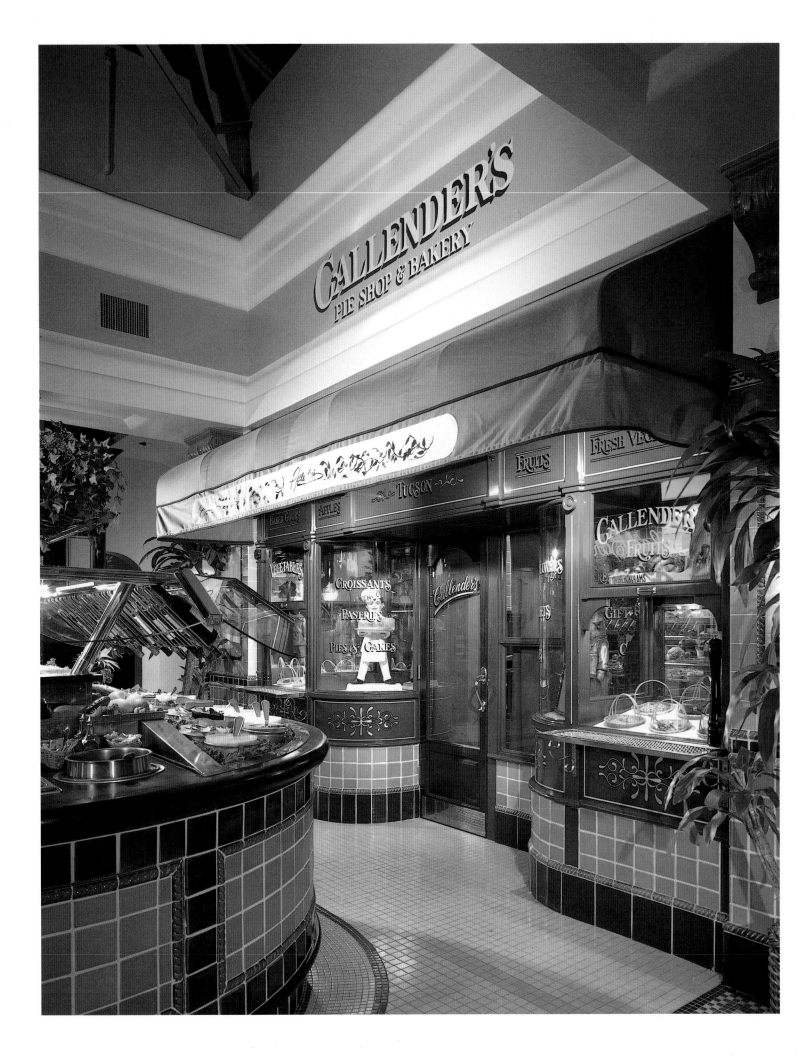

CAFES, CAFETERIAS AND COFFEE HOUSES

Cafe, Caffe and Cafeteria all start with "coffee" though more and more today coffee comes at the end — or with — the repast enjoyed in these comfortable, convivial, convenient, sometimes charming, but always casual dining places. Here, truly, what you see is what you eat. A Coffee House by any spelling in 19th century Europe featured coffee and tea and a vast and often elaborate selection of cakes, pastries, pies and tarts — all temptingly displayed on crystal stands trimmed with lace doilies or on trays lined with crisp, starched napkins. English tea rooms and Viennese Conditori abounded (and still abound) with cakes, scones, small sandwiches and whipped cream filled puffs. Whether in glass cases or on dessert wagons stationed around on the floor within easy viewing from any table, the tasty delicacy was and still is as important as the coffee or tea. Each coffee house was noted for and recommended by its special coffee blend — and the snacks that went with them. The French cafe, the Italian caffe, put the emphasis on the coffee, capuccino or espresso but prepared sandwiches were usually available. In places like Seattle, there is a trend towards the "pure" Cafe or Caffe with the major emphasis on the coffee but with a variety of blends and mixtures available sometimes you can even buy the freshly ground coffee to carry out. The cookies, muffins and biscuits, though not the star attraction, are effectively featured behind glass. Today's coffee house can provide anything from a morning eye opener to a quick break — an afternoon caffeine fix — or a way to while away an hour or so and watch the world go by.

A Cafe is defined as "a small and unpretentious restaurant or a barroom or cabaret" while a cafeteria is "a restaurant or dining room in which patrons wait on themselves carrying their food to their tables from counters where it is displayed and served, or a coffee shop." Some excellent examples of the self-service cafeterias are included in this chapter. They include the Soup Exchange, Bowman's Cafeteria, and The Feastery.

Though the food is visible on counters some restaurants offer service as well as self service, so after the patron has made a selection from the display of hot and cold choices, a server brings the selected foods to the seated diner. A self-service salad bar has also become a featured attraction to some restaurants and it is here that the presentation of food becomes the focal point of the design. Marie Callenders and Sizzler feature salad bars prominently in the restaurant layout. Bravo Cafe and Campus Cafe are what we traditionally think of as Coffee Shops where food is served simply, quickly and efficiently and a long counter with a display of food is the attention-getter and appetite whetter. Like Marie Callenders, Market City Cafe has a vast array of prepared foods-to-go up front that serve also as visual menus for diners.

Whether the diner orders coffee with the repast — after the snack or as the sole item — the coffee is more than just a thirst quencher. It is something to be savored and sipped — to relax with, to wind down with or to get picked-up by. In Boyds Coffee Shop, Starbucks and the Coffee Connection there is a choice of type or blend of coffee and though the shops are small and the seating areas are limited, the designs are beautifully done and there is a relaxed attitude about the ambience that seems to say "stay awhile and enjoy the moment." There are windows to look out of; to watch the parade going by in the street or in the mall where the coffee drinker can feel like a Continental people watcher.

Over two hundred years ago Charles Maurice de Tallyrand-Perigord wrote this about coffee:

> Black as the Devil
> Hot as Hell
> Pure as an Angel
> Sweet as Love.

The recipe is still effective and it tastes even better in the right setting with tempting tidbits surrounding the pot.

Marie Callender's
Tucson, AZ

MARIE CALLENDER'S

Tucson, AZ

Though this is an informal, seated dining room the diners are greeted by an array of prepared foods, packaged foods, and baked goods as soon as they enter into Marie Callender's. The selections are almost all there challenging the diner not to be tempted to try something at once from the appetizing display; usually they do wait till they leave to take some of the delicacies along with them.

The Marie Callender's chain is well known in the West and in Hawaii and this 11,000 sq. ft. operation is the most elaborate of the growing operation. While the basic Victorian theme, typical of all the Marie Callender's, is carried throughout the restaurant, the degree of elaboration and detail makes it unique with the space filled with brass, glass, architectural moldings, brick and ceramic tiles.

A conscious effort was made to reinforce the "homemade" fresh-baked-here concept. "The objective," the designer says, "was to create an atmosphere akin to being a guest in someone's home rather than a patron in a restaurant. To integrate food preparation and service with food consumption there is no sharp demarkation between 'public' and 'employee's only' spaces."

The salad bar, the fruit stand and the exciting Pie Shop, Bakery and Deli all add to the dining and take-out experience that is part of Marie Callender's.

Design: Beckham-Eisenman, Irvine, CA
Photographer: Milroy/McAleer, Newport Beach, CA

SOUP EXCHANGE

Oceanside, CA

The diner enters through a theatre marquee dotted with bright lights and sparkling with red illumination. Ahead, in full view, is food — glorious food! The architect/designer of this 10,000 sq. ft. space created a "grand boulevard" setting which depends upon over-scaled elements like poured-in-place curbing and specimen sized trees. The diners are immediately enveloped by the sharp, scintillating primary colors used on the ceramic tiles, the carpeting and the laminated surfaces. Overhead, the aluminum trussing was added to lower the effect of the high ceiling.

The 54', two-sided salad bar takes star billing in the theatrical ex-

travaganza and the neon lights provide an extra measure of sizzle to the signage while high intensity quartz lights illuminate the food service and dining areas. The tables and chairs are set to either side of the salad bar and here the illumination is gentler and the many plants in the space suggest a garden like setting.

According to Geoff Bechkam, the project's principal, "Our overriding objective was to create an environment where people would be motivated to walk around — enjoy the food displays — and sample more dishes. The key to the entire design is the lighting."

Design: Beckham & Eisenman, Irvine, CA
Photographer: Milroy/McAleer, Newport Beach, CA

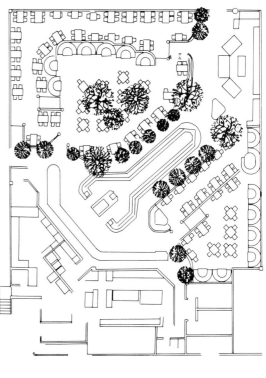

CAFFE ESPRIT

San Francisco, CA

Esprit has expanded its lifestyle concept to include a restaurant which is located adjacent to its factory outlet store in San Francisco. Bruce Slesinger, Esprit's in-house designer converted the original building, a grease garage, into an exciting cafe that combines "the best of American, Italian and Japanese design elements." It is Industrial Chic! The interior is light, open and spacious with seating on two levels. The high-tech interior is sleek and steely, neutral grays warmed with white ash for the high communal cafe tables and benches, and the specially designed Esprit-to-go packaging. As with everything Esprit, the graphic image is very discernable.

Large glass firehouse doors were added to extend the cafe to the outside garden where more tables are set under oversized canvas umbrellas along with the complementary landscaping. Inside the ceiling is lined up with rows of industrial type lamps and steely pendant lamps hang over the tables on the main level. The floor is gridded with giant size tiles of dark gray polished stone.

Design: Bruce Sleisinger of Esprit
Photographer: Sharon Risedorpf

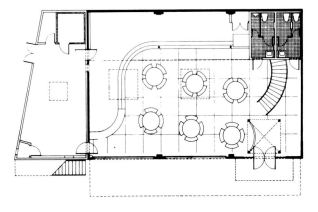

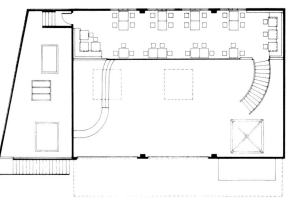

BOWMAN'S CAFETERIA

Schaumberg, IL

The cafeteria is located in an office complex where it mainly serves the tenants. Since the building's market position is at the upper end of the rental scale, the facility had to promote an image consistent with the quality of the complex. The cafeteria is on the concourse level which is a link between the two office towers and it also overlooks a pond which allows the outdoor patio adjacent to the pond to be used for dining space. The servery is situated in the center of the plan for better service and to promote an easy traffic flow. It also divides the space conveniently into smoking and non-smoking sections. Each section is thus more intimate — more personal scale. An octagonal platform is centered in each of the dining areas to "visually reduce and anchor these basically open spaces." The ceilings above the platforms are extended both above and below the adjacent ceiling plane and drywall lattice was created inside the coffers to support an indirect lighting scheme.

The freestanding kiosks for cold and hot food service allow circulation around their perimeters and neon graphics identify the general food categories. Surface mounted exposed bulb lighting adds a reflective shimmer to the service area.

The space is architecturally unified with a single wall covering and a monolithic synthetic stone material is used for bases and trim. The color scheme is limited to black, white, red and gray in assorted combinations, patterns and materials.

Design: Synectics Group, Chicago, IL
Photographer: Steinkamp/Ballogg Photographers

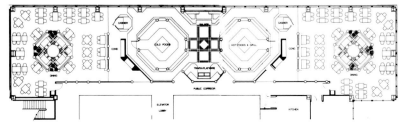

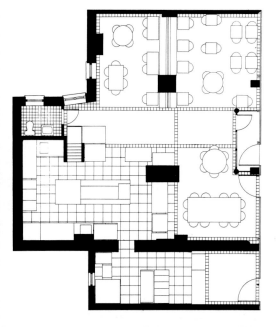

ANGELICA'S KITCHEN & BAKERY

New York, NY

The 15-year-old macrobiotic restaurant and bakery moved into a larger space, 2300 sq. ft. with a new glass facade, but the inside was sad; sloping concrete floors, peeling paint, exposed areas of brick on otherwise scruffy, uneven walls and a generally tired condition. Rather than "fix" it all up, and since the budget was very limited, the architect/designer opted to enhance the existing condition with a mixture of joint compounds and layers of paint "mottling" and texturing the wall surfaces — bringing out the "mediterranean-Greek Island" feeling that the owner, Leslie McEachern, "saw" in this lower East Side space.

The floors were resurfaced with tinted concrete and bordered with deep blue ceramic tiles and the same tiles were used on the floor in the very visible kitchen. The ceilings were "camouflaged" with an inexpensive cellulose fiber attenuating product. Because of the improvisational talent of the architect, L. Bogdanow and the unfailing assistance of a caring contractor, this low budget design has won top awards. The five large lighting fixtures were "designed" of parts and pieces picked up at local lamp stores and the wall sconces were "created" out of inexpensive wrought iron plant holders with blue glass bowls filled with beeswax. The mottled and textured treatment on the walls and columns and the eclectic mix of tables and chairs all add to the very personal look that is Angelica's Kitchen & Bakery.

Design: L. Bogdanow & Associates, NY
Contractor: David Elliot Construction Service, NY
Photographer: Daniel Eifert

STIXX CAFE

Baltimore, MD

Stixx Cafe is situated in a 1600 sq. ft. space in a retail shopping center in Baltimore. It was designed to seat 66 diners and the grill is the focal point set in the open dining room. A sweeping monocyclic plaster wall serves to separate this area from the back of the house and it also provides a neutral background for the gleaming metal and granite grill. The colorful dishes are prepared in full view of the diners and that is part of the entertainment for the evening. To highlight the theatrical aspect of the presentation a series of adjustable lights are focused on the "stage." A brilliant vermillion column adds a splotch of pure

color into the gray, neutral palette of the cafe's design which is further underscored with accents and areas of charcoal gray and black. All color has been minimized so that the visible food and the act of creation and presentation gets its full impact in the warmly lit interior.

The owner of the Cafe, Tzu Ming Yang, was responsible for the faux finish on the table tops while Valley Craftsmen created the faux finishes on the walls. The vertical surface of the counters are surfaced with copper.

Design: Hord, Coplan, Macht, Inc., Baltimore, MD
Photographer: Brough Schamp

THE FEASTERY

Rosslyn, VA

The 207-seat fast food restaurant is located in a Virginia shopping mall where it competes for breakfast and luncheon business so service must be efficient — and fast. Marc Reshefsky, the architect, had to turn this oddly shaped L space of 5800 sq. ft. into something "upscaled and classy" with a touch of today — and a smattering of Memphis. "Initially, the bright lights, colors and patterns attracted the mall shoppers," and so the architect added plastic enclosed strings of bee lights along the turquoise beams that traverse the ceiling, and around the signage. Yellow spheres serve as caps on the yellow and white striped Memphisian columns that appear as a grid upon the floor plan and they flank the main entrance into the Feastery as well as into the main seating area. Checkerboarded borders of yellow and white ceramic tiles not only serve to indicate the traffic patterns and divide up the space, they are also repeated on the counters and the partitions between the seating areas. Contemporary black and white lattice panels serve as see-through screens that separate areas but do not hide them. The entire floor is paved with white ceramic tiles patterned with the checkerboard borders. The plastic laminated surfaces contribute to the low maintenance requirements of the equipment and the furnishings.

Design: MR + A Architects, Bethesda, MD
Photographer: Andrew Lautman

BRAVO CAFE

Willowbrook Mall, Wayne, NJ

It is all theater in this operation where freshly made pizzas take top billing. The ovens are on view and displayed in the glass cases all along the counter there is a colorful and well lit presentation of the many toppings; the cheeses, meats, tomatoes and other vegetables. Overhead swing swollen provolone cheeses girdled in twine, salamis, strings of garlic, peppers and onions. The dough is freshly pressed, kneaded and tossed in view of the diners and a custom burnished brass hood adds an extra dash of glitz to the food festivities going on under the rows of incandescent floods and spots.

Design: Martin Dorf Associates, NY

CAMPUS CAFE

Parsippany, NJ

Another Pizza Parlor but this one is located in an office building. Here "Personal Pedigree 9" Pizzas" are prepared in full view of the customers who can watch them being placed in a conveyor pizza oven. In addition, at other very visible stations, as shown here, the diner can get salads, sandwiches, soups and pastas and each area is clearly signed on the signage band that runs overhead. Trays are available at each station. High intensity, color corrected low voltage lighting enhances the color of the foods. Warm cherry wood and white corian tops add to the sense of quality and up-scales the Campus Cafe visually.

Design: Martin Dorf Associates, NY

SIZZLER

Bellflower, CA

This nationwide chain of steak and salad restaurants gets a happy new expression in Bellflower, California. The peach-toned wood beams and ceiling trusses and the whole barn-like construction as well as the sloping fins that define the sloping ceiling all supply a contemporary "Western" look. The Western look is usually associated with steaks and Sizzler. Here, however, it is an updated Southwestern feeling executed in a sophisticated palette of peach, aqua and turquoise with natural oak detailing and complements. The wood chairs are rubbed with peach as are the round columns capped with layers of cool colors. The carpeting is teal colored in the dining area and under the salad bar and the self-service area the floor is finished with white ceramic squares dotted in turquoise. The Southwest color scheme comes together on the design on the tiled salad bar and in the upholstery used on the banquettes. Even the bright neon signs carry through the established color scheme. Overhead giant air ducts are painted a happy turquoise color while below all the greenery brings the outdoors inside.

Design: Muzingo Associates, Los Angeles, CA
Principal: Gina Muzingo
Photographs: Peter Malinowski

MARKET CITY CAFE

Pasadena, CA

The relaxed, easy-going, easy-to-look-at Cafe is located in historic downtown Pasadena. Upon entering into the cool dimness of the restaurant the patron is greeted with food; prepared foods, salads, fresh fruits and vegetables and assorted imported packaged delicacies. Samuel Pastron, the grandfather of one of the owners, helped with the "interior decorating and display" of this part of the cafe. "He was in the grocery business all his life and the design for all the produce you see here is his. He wouldn't let us forget the 100% extra virgin olive oil either, and the balsamic vinegars and the prosciutto, California cheeses and the finest and freshest produce available."

The heritage and cooking traditions of two Napolitana grandmothers and 22 uncles and aunts are combined in the menu along with the deft contemporary contributions of the two owners. After the original onslaught of the well displayed foods the diner can choose to sit in the homey and roomy brick, wood and ceramic tiled dining room or venture out into the semi-enclosed garden and enjoy life and food under the canvas umbrellas surrounded by statuary, plants and trees. On the menu there is a reminder: "Our food travels — Take-it-to-go.'"

Architects: Architects Consortium, Los Angeles, CA
Design/Owners: Sal Casolo and Chipper Pastron
Photographer: Father & Suns

BOYD'S COFFEE SHOP

Portland, OR

This is a prototype design for the Boyd's Coffee Company and it is aimed at Seattle's quality conscious coffee consumers. The 90-year-old company wanted to distinguish itself from the usual Euro/Italian coffee shop image and the Wyatt, Stapper Architects were called in to make the new look appear.

The focal point in the 600 sq. ft. space is a barista station banded with brass and stainless steel. This barista station "alludes to the aesthetics of coffee roasting and likewise celebrates the process of making an espresso drink by bringing it up front rather than hiding it behind the counter."

The up-scaled design reaffirms the American background of the company and the materials and details are sophisticated yet "solid and established." The store's interior is wrapped with dark stained mahogany offset with brass and stainless steel accents. Set into the terazzo floor are brass inlays which radiate out from the barista station in concentric circles. The custom casework, wainscotting and millwork are enhanced by the low voltage display lights as is the modular grid system which holds a display of coffee beans in clear acrylic bins along with photographs, menu-graphics and assorted Boyd memorabalia. This is a place for a relaxing cup of special coffee — or the place to buy the beans and the coffee making equipment.

Design: Wyatt, Stapper Architects, Seattle, WA
Photos: Robert Pisano, Seattle, WA

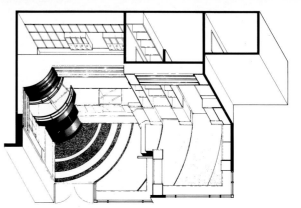

STARBUCK'S COFFEE STORE

West Pacific Center, Seattle, WA

In a space of less than 400 sq. ft. the architects created an "up-scale version of its successful coffee bar and retail store" for this high end downtown location. Starbuck's is a premier roasting company and they are planning to open more of these small, friendly — and convenient shops where coffee aficionados can enjoy a cup of specially brewed coffee from a selection of blends — or can buy the ground beans.

The walls are mottled in gray to simulate stone or granite and the bar is covered with a black laminate trimmed with stainless steel. Black ceramic tiles are laid on the floor and frosted glass drop lights follow the contour of the angling bar. The facade is glass and gray granite and green lights behind the stainless steel fascia creates a vibrant background for the shop's cut out letters. The illuminated circular logos are also done in green and white.

Design: The Callison Partnership, Seattle, WA
Photographer: Thomas Harris, Seattle, WA

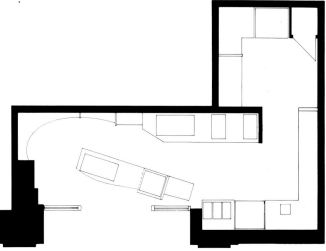

THE COFFEE CONNECTION

Boston, MA

The 300 sq. ft. mini-bar was designed with the efficiency of a machine. The plan evolved around the plumbing, the equipment and the circulation pattern — and everything had to be within reach of the server. Located in the lobby of one of Boston's prestigious office towers, the "machine" is constructed of fine woods and marbles in respect to the architecture around it. The curved layout of the handsome wood bar "allows the server to be the focus for the customer at the front counter and the pivot point for the work station behind."

Design: Schwartz/Silver, Boston, MA
Photographer: Richard Mandelkorn, Newton, MA

ORANGE STREET TEA SHOP

Lancaster, PA

When walking along on an old brick paved street in a lovely old town that is gently mellowing this is the kind of shop you would hope to find for a relaxing yet bracing cup of tea. The building is old but the fixtures and cabinetry is far older. Original pieces of retail furniture were carefully removed from 18th century and 19th century establishments — lovingly restored and set up to fill the needs of this shop. Originally it began as a retail source for teas, coffees, herbs, spices and related housewares but over a few years it became a tea shop/restaurant and there is now a full service restaurant located in the basement.

The floors are paved with bricks and a long, old wooden counter faced with ancient metal and wood bar stools is used to serve up a cup of coffee or tea, or for the shopper to perch on while making taste-affecting decisions. Ceilings are naturally low and white milk-glass globes in the shop provide soft, low-keyed lighting that is so right with the soft, faded colors of the ambience.

In the dining area, brass and copper lanterns and wall sconces offer gentle illumination. When the fire is lit in the fireplace, who could ask for more? Orange St. Tea Shop is a delightful stroll into the past with all the convenience of today.

Owner/Designer: Elvin Hess, Lancaster, PA

DINERS, DELIS AND DELI-DINING

Delis and Diners have a common denominator and that is nostalgia. They share a remembrance of things past when food was simple, wholesome and uncomplicated and when there seemed to be an innocence in the world. The deli or delicatessen of old was actually a forerunner to today's "gourmet-to-go." It was filled with smells and sights that stimulated the salivary glands; imported sausages, salamis and wursts — cheeses from foreign lands and wonderful packaged delicacies from exotic places — food you just didn't find in the corner grocery or the big A&P down the road. While a red-cheeked, braided and buxom "momma" puttered about in the rear kitchen preparing hot potato salad, baking and basting hams and turkeys and stirring pots of bubbling brews to go, Poppa in white apron and straw hat (no matter what the season) and sleeves caught up in fanciful arm garters ruled behind the spotlessly clean, gleaming glass counters ladened with salads, meats, cold cuts and imported specialties. That is how we "remember" the old deli of the early part of the twentieth century; a place of warmth, friendliness, concern for customers and wonderful foods all prepared and ready to take. Today's delis may have to do without the costumed momma and poppa, the sawdusted floors, the marble counters, the whirring fans but the smells and sights are still there and there is more to see and smell than ever before. Shelves are filled with rows and rows of imported cans and packages of specialty foods and the glass showcases burst with gourmet delights usually fanciful and imaginative than momma's hams, salads and puddings.

Although the warmth and charm of oak shelves and fixtured interiors — the patterned tin ceilings and the homey feeling is still present in new delis — there is a difference. Today you can have your pate and eat it too. Delis come with dining rooms where the hungry or just the tempted can fill up on some of the delicacies and still carry more home to enjoy at a later time. It is like the old conundrum: what came first, the chicken or the egg? Did the deli become so popular and the food, so lovingly presented, become so desirable that customers needed instant satisfaction and thus the dining area was born or was the food in the restaurant so great that the demand arose for more to take out and the deli became a featured adjunct to the restaurant. In our selections like the Stage Deli, Convito Italiano, and Vivande Porta Via, to name a few, we draw no conclusions as to "the chicken or the egg" but what is obvious is that the deli area is almost always up front and to tempt the hungry with an unending smorgasbord of prepared and packaged foods — under warm and flattering lights in an ambience filled with "gemutlischkeit."

The Diner is pure nostalgia and, interestingly, the appeal is often more to those who were not yet born, or much too young to really remember, the originals. Black and white tiled floors, patterned, chromed panels and counter fronts, red naughahyde benches, neon streamers reflecting in the Streamline Moderne panels and the sight of hamburgers being grilled, sandwiches being stacked and malteds being mixed is entertainment for all the senses. It is "American Grafitti" on a double feature bill with "Diner," and it is a reflection of a period of peace and prosperity, innocence, simple pleasures and little thought of what the future has in store. In our selection of Diners we run the gamut from the truly casual "hamburger joint" of the '50s like Johnny Rocket in Los Angeles to the more upscaled dining diners of the Rose City Diner and Edies Diner in Pasadena. The Broadway Diner in Santa Monica is the "in" dining place and it is new, sleek and sophisticated plus it encompasses a market, a gourmet-to-go, and a wine shop in its total design. The emphasis is always on fun and food being prepared in sight of the diner and the ambience created by the designers/architects enhances the total experience whether it is eating in — or taking out — or both.

Rose City Diner
Pasadena, CA

ROSE CITY DINER

Pasadena, CA

Located in old Pasadena, only a few stores down from the Market City Cafe, is this 4500 sq. ft. Rose City Diner which is designed as a "tribute to the historically rich town in a setting that is pure 50s." From the black and white checkerboarded floor to the small black and white ceramic tiles that are patterned into a footrest for the rosy pink soda fountain to the dropped globe lights overhead the design is filled with memories and memorabilia — and with art deco details. The color palette is mainly limited to rose-pinks, black and white and lots of sleek and shiny chrome accents like the patterned fascia over the soda fountain. The furnishings and fixtures throughout are reminders of another time and antique accessories like a Schwinn bike, a Mobil Gas pump and even the un-trustworthy enameled step-on scale all add to the diner's "authenticity." As a final acknowledgment to Pasadena's place in the 50s there are photographs of the Rose Parades and Rose Queens of that period along with timely cliches painted on for fun reading.

Design: Schafer Associates, Oakbrook Terrace, IL
Photographer: Milroy/McAleer, Costa Mesa, CA

EDIE'S DINER

Pasadena, CA

Pasadena, like Los Angeles, won't let go of the 50s — or the diners. The same designers that gave us the Rose City Diner came up with this one which is complete with table side juke boxes and bubblegum smacking waitresses. The exterior facade elements introduce the lineal "dining car" look with polished stainless steel trim and panels, glass blocks, and a backlit awning. Inside — the 50s lives again! The streamlined linear layout of the pullman style booth seating is detailed with tuck and rolled backs, upholstered in appropriate, of-the-period mottled red vinyl. The "black granite" laminate tops have the classic stainless steel edge detailing and hanging light fixtures, researched and carefully selected, add character to the design along with the black and white checkerboarded vinyl floor. Custom stainless steel doors, panels and coat racks make their impact on the total scene while coating it with more nostalgia.

Design: Schafer Associates, Oakbrook Terrace, IL
Photographer: Milroy/McAleer, Costa Mesa, CA

JOHNNY ROCKET

Los Angeles, CA

The Johnny Rocket diners, in look and in service, return to the 30s and 40s when hamburger stands could be found on any neighborhood corner or busy downtown thoroughfare and fresh, tasty food was served in a friendly and inviting atmosphere. This, the first of the Johnny Rockets, opened in 1986 and has since been cloned in Beverly Hills, Chicago, Atlanta and even Tokyo. The exterior fondly reminds one of the old White Towers of cherished memories — all sheathed in white horizontally striped with strips of chrome and underscored with bands of neon. Inside just about everything is white enamel or laminate or ceramic tile otherwise it is chrome trim or patterned panels of the silvery gray material. The red vinyl bar stools are perched on gleaming rods of steel bolted down to the mini-tiled floor. Individual juke boxes dot the black topped dispensers and the salt and pepper shakers. All the food is prepared to order and in full view of the diners on a service table just beyond the counters and on the griddles under the chromed panels on the rear wall. For those who care to breathe the Melrose Ave. traffic fumes there is a pleasant outdoor seating area.

Architect: Sherrod Marshall, AIA, Los Angeles, CA
Photographer: Father & Suns

RALPHIES DINER

Baltimore, MD

Maybe not the actual setting for the movie "Diner" but close enough. Ralphies Diner is also set in Baltimore though the name is more likely to bring back memories of Ralph and Norton. It was created to "appeal to the age group from 8 to 80" and the space is designed to be kind and generous to the patrons.

Large square panels of glass let the outdoor light flood in over the black and white ceramic tiled floor and the furniture and fixtures made of mahogany, birdseye maple, and satin aluminum. Bistro furniture is added to make the space seem more inviting and exciting and the warm incandescent illumination does make things look warm and friendly. The use of vaulted cove lit ceilings creates definition for the dining spaces. A special soda fountain area was created for those who crave desserts and up front, for those who can be tempted, the baked goods is displayed for take-out at the cashier's counter.

Design: Martin Dorf Associates, NY

BIG ED'S DINER / DELI

Honolulu, HI

Diner Hawaiian Style! The Ward Center is a new shopping plaza just past the giant Ala Moana Mall — on the way to the airport and it is gaining a following among the "natives" who want good things in fairly quiet surroundings. The hanger-like structure that contains Big Ed's all but vanishes since all the light and interest is kept below on the food presentation and the cozy, wood-filled ambience. The counters and serving areas are made of rich, deep brown stained woods and the airducts, decorative valances and interior awnings are in Pompeiian red. Part of the floor is tiled with terra cotta squares while the bar area reminds one of what a turn-of-the-century local bar must have looked like with the mini-tiled floor and the brass railing and ball decorations. However, very contemporary lighting fixtures extend down from somewhere on high — on fixed rods — to light up the area. In other parts of Big Ed's, milkglass globes on short stems shade the incandescent lamps that send flattering light down on to food and diners alike.

Design: Media Five, Honolulu, HI
Photographer: David Franzen

L.A. DINER (OASIS DINER)

Boulder, CO

At night the Oasis Diner (now renamed the L.A. Diner) lights up the street with its blaze of neon catching and reflecting off every bit of patterned steel panels and chrome striping. Over the door the stepped-up, art deco, design is outlined in neon. Inside things are slick, shiny and Streamline Moderne. The coffee urn area with the embedded clock and the sunray design pressed into the shimmering chrome panel probably best defines the look and essence of this diner. In the dining section black vinyl upholstered seats blend with the soft gray walls, and the table tops are wood finished and edged with stainless steel like the framed period prints and the wall sconces between the booths.

The main, centrally located counter consists of consecutive bands of brushed steel stepping down, tier by tier, to meet the set back wood veneered base. The utter symmetry of the design and composition suggest the time-frame of the diner's inspiration.

Design: Communication Arts Inc., Boulder, CO
Photographer: Geoffrey Wheeler & Kim Michael Puliti

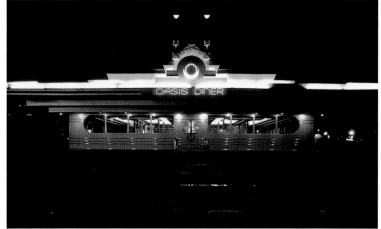

BROADWAY DINER

Santa Monica, CA

Steven Ehrlich has created "an urban marketplace attuned to the 1990s." Outside a sidewalk cafe beckons to the strollers on the 3rd St. pedestrian mall and inside is a bustling food emporium/restaurant which has been arranged into specialty "neighborhoods" which include a market, a delicatessen, a wine room, bar, open kitchen, dining counter and restaurant. The open floor plan turns the 10,000 sq. ft. space into a "village fair" where shoppers and diners can not only enjoy watching the chefs in the kitchen and the bakers at the ovens but also the people parade going by. "Using materials such as tinted plywoods, colored concretes, stainless steel, glass and natural woods, I achieved a new contemporary space based on NY and European delis I studied," says Steven Ehrlich. *The L.A. Times,* reporting on the Broadway Deli, said "to shop the Broadway Deli is to enter a world in which grocery shopping is elevated from an errand into a cultural event," and since the architect grounds his designs in the cultural anthropology of L.A. — "a marketplace celebrates the city's rich mix of peoples." This is the place to see and meet the people.

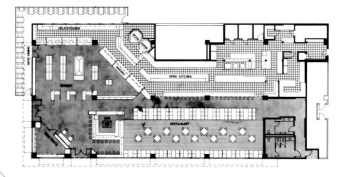

Design: Steven D. Ehrlich, AIA, Venice, CA
Photographer: Tom Bonner, Venica, CA

ISAAC'S DELI

Greenfield Corp. Center, Lancaster, PA

Isaac's is a growing chain of local quick service deli/restaurants and the team of Hickey and Hess have established a signature image for the developing chain. Though each operation differs from the others there are certain recognizable design elements that reaffirm the Isaac's identity. Some delis are located in renovated, historic houses but the designers have avoided trite regional motifs. Each location is treated as a new project though they are all contemporary, fresh, and mostly done in neutral schemes highlighted with glass blocks, sweeping curved lines and always the open kitchens.

This high-tech 4200 sq. ft. space at Greenfield is filled with air vents and ducts painted charcoal gray and a wide curving band outlined with red neon that sweeps through the dining space defining the mezzanine level which follows the same curved line. A wall of glass blocks finishes the cyma-recta movement of overhead band. The interior is done in gray, white and black with natural woods and shots of red to brighten up the ambience.

Design: Kaufman Hickey Architects, Lancaster, PA
Principal: Carol Hickey, R.A.
Design: Eloin Hess
Photographer: John Hess, Lancaster, PA

ISAAC'S DELI

Centerville Rd., Lancaster, PA

Up front at this 3600 sq. ft. Isaac's Deli the shopper is faced with prepared foods on display. The entire floor area is covered with a checkerboard of black and white vinyl tiles and the sitting area is carpeted with a dark gray commercial twist. The white walls are tinted by the cool blue uplights and mulberry, deep rose and dark red have been added to the unusual neutral color scheme. The deep red/purple colored tubes or columns serve as dividers and architectural separators and the elevated dining area is marked off with metal pipe railing of the same color. lattice-work of a deep teal color is used throughout as a decorative motif, like the column, and can be seen used as a background for the natural oak seating units which are also trimmed with teal. The average seating capacity for each Isaac's Deli is about 130 persons and each outlet has an impressive take-out selection.

Design: Kaufman Hickey, Lancaster, PA
Principal: Carol Hickey, R.A.
Design: Elvin Hess
Photographer: John Hess

KATZ'S DELI

Toronto, Ont., Canada

The architects/designers have taken a bright, bold and very colorful step in creating this contemporary styled Deli with an old fashioned name. The space is rich in wonderful, stinging colors; walls are painted tomato red or shocking pink, air ducts are finished in green and food counters are rosy red overlaid with white grids. The floors are marked off and traffic patterns are identified by the neutral gray vinyl material contrasting with the earth brown carpeting. Not to be omitted, — natural woods of a honey gold color are used to construct the post and lintel element on the floor that divides the large open space into smaller more intimate and more specialized areas. Chairs are finished in bright green and bands of blue-violet accentuate the upholstered chair backs and outline the dwarf partitions and dividers. Droplights with enameled metal shades hang from the dark ceiling to light up the dining space.

Design: Hirschberg Design Group, Toronto, Ont., Canada
Photographer: David Whittaker

HAROLD'S N.Y. DELI

Rancho, CA

Harold's is a prototype for a new kind of quick service chain restaurant that would be suitable in suburban neighborhoods or in high density metropolises. Harold's regresses to a 1930s look — "American Depression Folklore" — with an upbeat feeling.

A very important part of creating the desired ambience is the specially commissioned murals of N.Y. street scenes. They are placed high on the wall — where windows would be if there were windows. Black silhouettes were made and created into a fin which penetrates the amber lighting from below and seem to reflect onto the "N.Y. streets." "It is as though one were watching from below street level," says Gina Muzingo. The cashier's station was built around a problem column and now customers are directed through the bakery and the deli before they are seated — smelling and touching the products. They are encouraged to return on their way out to buy something to take with them.

The flooring material is plywood endgrain which is both durable and attractive and was used in factories back in the 30s. Tambour wood strips are used decoratively on the counters, on walls and as a frieze under the ceiling. Through the designer, Harold's has found the sunny side of the 30s street.

Design: Muzingo Associates, Los Angeles, CA
Principal: Gina Muzingo
Artist: Bruce Tunis
Architect: Kwang Cook, Arch.
Photographer: Grey Crawford

CANDY'S III

New York, NY

This food operation needed to be ambidexterous. During the day it had to serve people in a hurry — who rushed in to eat quickly, cafeteria style. But, at sundown things change in arty Soho and the design had to accommodate for a quick conversion to a full service dining room in keeping with the up temp ambience of the neighborhood. The solution was to divide the restaurant almost in half by using display refrigerators surrounded by an illuminated glass block wall as the dividing partition. The refrigerators open up to the take-out side of Candy's III. For atmosphere the designers, Fred Fox and Samuel Arlen, decided on a theme of Soho in "ruin." "Crumbling" rusticated walls were created out of alternating bands of terra cotta and beige laminates. Through these "ruins" the diner catches glimpses of historical scenes which are actually photographic collages papered onto the walls. The ragged painted plywood at the top adds to the illusion of walls being ripped away and the suspended broken columns that project down from the ceiling reinforce the effect.

Throughout, the floor is laid in a checkerboard pattern compos-

ed of small black and white tiles and the terra-cotta and beige color scheme is carried through on the Deli side as well. The lighting is from recessed spots in the ceiling and from up lights atop the floating octagonal column caps.

Design: Arlen & Fox, Architects, NY
Photographer: James D'Addio

STAGE DELI

New York, NY

In honor of its 50th anniversary, this "landmarked" Broadway Deli underwent a major renovation. The owners wanted a light and airy atmosphere but they still wanted to retain the old time flavor that made this an "institution" and a hangout for deli-mavens. In place of the dingy sidewalk cafe in went an all glass greenhouse with lighting effects to evoke the art deco style of the 30s. This was accomplished by designing special frosted ribbed glass lighting units that defined the contours of the greenhouse structure at night. To further emphasize the effect, frosted step-

ped pendant light fixtures were used over the tables. The same glass lighting units were used to frame the photo collage of the many stars of stage, screen, sports, radio and TV who frequent — or had frequented — the Stage Deli in its illustrious past. To bring the past into the present the mahogany panelled bar, antique peach toned walls and ceramic tiled floors were added into the design of the space along with the low keyed lighting, the red table tops and the dark green leather-like, upholstered chair seats.

Design: Arlen/Fox, Architects, NY
Photographer: James D'Addio

EMBASSY GOURMET

New York, NY

This Deli/Restaurant was originally conceived as a series of shops-within-the-shop in which one could purchase delicacies, a sandwich, a salad, and then have the option of taking the food out or eating it in the rear dining room. The difficulty the architects faced was the long narrow space of the shop which meant that the dining room would be completely hidden in the rear. The solution was to devise a series of neon banded arches which would serve as signs and partitions; they would identify the assorted specialty shops below while they visually stretched the narrow space. At the same time they would serve as magnets to draw people back into the space and into the dining area.

To open up the relatively small dining area, Fox and Arlen optically enlarged the space by introducing a series of arched mirror "windows" that helped stretch the space with reflections. The pleasant peach colored walls and the dynamic checkerboard floor below also help create a sense of space as do the light scaled ice-cream chairs with their red upholstered seats.

Design: Arlen/Fox, Architects, NY
Photographer: James A'Addio

PEGGY FOWLER, CATERER

Akron, OH

In a relatively small space there is a lot going on and the designer was able to visually open up the space to accommodate Ms. Fowler's many requirements. In addition to the all-important catering service there is a complete line of take home foods which have to be displayed. All these specialties can be enjoyed in the Petit Cafe which is open during the regular kitchen hours and it serves a quick light breakfast, a full lunch or an anytime break, when one can savor the food on view.

The space is decorated in black and white, patterned with a checkerboard design and highlighted with bright red. The ribbed opalescent pendant lamps combine with the fluorescents in the dropped ceiling to illuminate the foods on display and the metallic cooking equipment that glistens in the open kitchen area. Peggy Fowler's compact operation also prepares "in-box" meals-to-go, sandwich and salad trays, as well as food gifts on order.

Design: F. Eugene Smith/Design Management, Akron, OH

CONVITO ITALIANO

Chestnut Galleria, Chicago, IL

Convito Italiano is a restaurant, a cafe, a specialty deli and prepared foods "emporium" as well as a catering service. This, the second and newest of the Convito Italiano operations, covers 10,000 sq. ft. on two levels and an attractive open staircase leads from the retail level where shelves are neatly stacked and displays abound in baskets set on the floor — on counters and wherever the shopper can be introduced to the packaged and prepared foods up to the second level. Here is located the restaurant with 65 seats open for lunch and dinner and a wine bar that serves a wide selection of Italian wines by the glass. The operation also includes a 40 seat outdoor cafe and a 30 seat indoor one.

The food inventory includes approximately 75 cheeses, 500 grocery items, and a daily selection from the 100 hot dishes and 150 salads in Convito's repitoire. There is also an inventory of over 1000 labels of imported Italian wines. "I wanted to bring all the shops I found in Italy under one roof," says Nancy Barocci the owner and she has succeeded within the space she has, since there is a Salumeria (deli), a Drogheria (grocery), a Pasta e Salsa (pasta and sauces), a Cantina (wine shop), Rosticceria (hot prepared foods) and a Panneteria (bakery). Convito means "everything that goes into the feast" and everything is here and on display in the clear, crisp, Milanese-inspired white, chrome and glass interior — with touches of post-modernism.

Display Designer: Sharon Evans Rager
Photographs: Tony Romano, Chicago

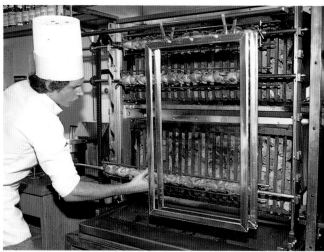

VIVANDE PORTA VIA

San Francisco, CA

What began as a gourmet take-out delicatessen which only included a few tables for those who could not wait to sample the culinary delights prepared by the outstanding chef/author/ food consultant/ and instructor to professional chefs, Carlo Middione — has now become a specialty food store/restaurant. The name tells the first part of the story — "foods to be taken away," and the Diner's Club magazine has dubbed this "one of the ultimate delis in the world along with Pecks of Milan, Fauchon of Paris and Dallmayer in Munich."

The store is 25' wide by 75' long and one long side wall is exposed red brick overlaid with ceramic pigs' heads, personal decorative objects and filled garden baskets. Covered tables to seat the lucky 40 patrons are snuggled up along this wall. Up front, is the store's retail presentation. Four giant refrigerator cases show off meats, cheeses, cold prepared foods, salads, and pastries. Behind, on shelves, are the cans and jars filled with imported specialties. There is a separate area devoted to imported oils, vinegars and condiments just inside the front door. A row of stools, farther back, face a counter for "fast service" which also provides a complete "floor show"; here is where pasta is prepared and the baking is done. From the Espresso Bar, a sit-down area beyond the restaurant, the coffee sipper has an open view into the kitchen where Chef Middione and his staff of top chefs work over steaming pots and a wall of roasters.

"People get so turned on seeing food being prepared. Like Ballet or Theater — it is a performing art; there is movement, shape, form, timing and balance," says Elizabeth Middione. At Vivande Porta Via there is good food — and entertainment.

Architect: Fogel & Lynch, Peaks Island, ME
Graphic Design: Betty Duke
Designer/Owner: Elizabeth Middione

SWINGING SOUTH

Memphis International Airport, Memphis, TN

"We found that in active airport situations there are several ways to get the traveler's attention. The use of vibrant colors, locating abundant food displays close to the concourse area, signage, neon and the use of reflective materials — all combined with a good theme design — presents an attractive choice for the travelers as well as the meeters and greeters."

The interior of this deli/bar is warm, bright and cheerful. From the gridded floor of black granite up the creamy walls to the wide slashes of red painted pick wood wainscotting and the sizzling neon signage — the space is contemporary with suggestions of designs past like the semi-dividing wall of glass blocks. Fresh

food is displayed up front in a shiny white refrigerated case and the colorful arrangement is mirrored in the dropped reflective stainless steel surfaced area over the case. The black and beige checkerboard pattern wraps itself around counter enclosures on the neutral carpeted floor and it takes over the whole wall behind the red bar with the black upholstered chairs. In this area the floor is patterned in black and white but the white squares are framed in black rather than checkered. A period jukebox is added to provide some of that "neighborhood spot" atmosphere to Swinging South.

Design: DiLeonardo International, Warwick, RI
Artwork: Jessica Shotz, Artisrey, Brockton, MA
Photographer: Warren Jagger

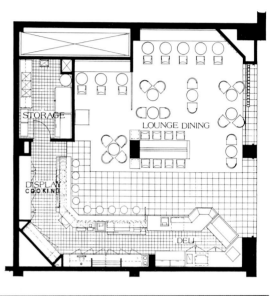

AERO PLACE

Dayton Airport, Dayton, OH

This Dobb's operation is located in another airport and the same architect/design team brings a different look to this deli/bar. The color scheme in Aero Place is mainly gray and white; the floor is tiled with small white ceramic tiles divided into larger squares and bordered with strips and panels of gray tiles. Rich wood veneers provide some extra warmth to the area's flushed white wall surfaces. The wood appears on the bar top, on facing counters, and on dwarf dividers on the floor. The food, ready to-go or to be eaten here, is presented in glass fronted, self-illuminated cases and hanging over them are white metal dome pendants which add incandescent highlights to the prepared foods below. Light scaled black metal chairs and tables are conveniently located nearby for those who would eat in. Fluorescent ceiling washers "cool" off the upper stretches of space while the incandescents supply the peachy glow over the tables. Flashes of neon, on signs and on logo plaques, add spice to the setting.

Design: Di Leonardo International, Warwick, RI

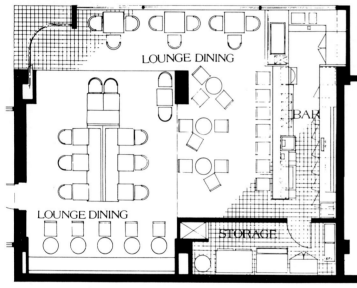

SWEETWATER'S

Memphis International Airport, Memphis, TN

Located in the same food court as Swinging South and designed by the same architects is Sweetwater's, a Dobb's operation. More "up-scaled" than the latter, the designers opted for subdued colors, intimate lighting and a liberal amount of glass and mirror to visually expand the relatively small space. A series of fragmented pop art classics provide a liveliness while echoing the gridwork of the paneling, the ironwork, and the etched glass. The natural wood used in the gridwork also appears in moldings and fascia bands — all adding to the character of the gray/mauve color scheme. The black gridwork on the front glass sort of divides the diners inside from the traffic on the concourse.

A solid gray granite shucking and seafood display station shows off the fresh foods under strong, clear light and the station is framed with stainless steel for a reflective, high-tech look.

The designers have used color and light to "create a welcome oasis for the traveler" and quality materials and original artwork tells the traveler that he/she is as special as the space that has been designed for his/her pleasure.

Design: DiLeonardo International, Warwick, RI
Artwork: Jessica Sholz, Artisrey, Brockton, MA
Photographer: Warren Jagger

GRILLS AND GROOVY PLACES

It is all theater! It's make-believe — it's magic and it's mouth-watering. With a cast of food ready to make an appearance on stage (or on the plate) and the audience is part of the ensuing drama — or comedy — that is about to be performed. It is theater-in-the-round or in the square and the diners are part of the act. It is a fun version of the Japanese tea ceremony — but with food.

In each of our chapters the reader can see how, as we start the last decade of this century, we have become more International-ized — more sophisticated — more globally aware in our tastes and appetites. Thai food and Moroccan delicacies are no longer reserved for only those lucky few who have passports to travel to faraway places. The exotic and unique has become familiar but it hasn't lost its glamour. What the beat, beat, beat of the pizza is in a fast food operation is the slap, slap, slap of the tortilla in the charm-filled Mexican "cantina" or the flick, flick, flick of the fish knife in the hands of the red headbanded sushi chef behind the serving bar in the Japanese restaurant. In this chapter it is the prepara-tion of the food rather than the fully prepared foods that are the star attractions and, again, it is the stage setting that is so vital to the presentation of the food. Like a good set design, it takes color and light to create the proper illusion and to forward the action, — enough lights on the central characters (the food and the cooks) and shadows on the audience to enhance the mystery and marvel of what is about to un-fold — what is to be created before their very eyes. Some restaurants in this chapter put their stage center and seat the audience around it. Others elevate the scene of the ac-tion so that the diners can be entertained all the while they are sipping and supping. In still other instances, the play takes place up front — near the entrance — as an overture to the whole dining experience that is about to follow. The smoky smells that emanate from the charcoal grill that might be treated with mesquite chips is like a musical background for the nose instead of the ear, and can any magician be more adept or fascile than the maitre d' tossing a Caesar salad with parsley, pepper and panache? Costumes can be corny but they can also be clever and fun. Teriyaki is so much more Japanese when served by a kimono-clad waitress pitter-pattering about in her soft black slippers just as a hamburger can taste better when wheeled in by a sunbleached surfer on roller skates. It is all in the act!

In this chapter we touch on some of these International-style show places as well as purely American settings and as may be ex-pected some of the most theatrical ventures are out on the West Coast. Chopsticks features "healthy" Oriental-style food and it is prepared in full view of the diners seated along the long bar while the young whizzing kids that enter your orders in their hand held computers provide entertainment as well. Brandy Ho adds a new dimension to elegant Chinese dining and here the spectacle is set behind a proscenium of lights and under a roof of illuminated green tiles and the stage is located in such a way that those who wish to, can watch the progress in the prepara-tion of their meal. California Beach Rock 'N' Sushi is clever and imaginative; a fun-filled space rich in color and forms. The Knollwood operations are giant stage sets upon which we — the hungry players play our part amidst the trappings and memorabilia of times gone by but fondly remembered. Coconut Grill would have you swept away to a jungle playland or a tropic isle where the expert cooks perform in the open-for-viewing kitchen framed with louvered shutters. Pappa's Grill brings you the glories of Greece in a smartly updated, multi-leveled setting where the focal point of the place is the food preparation area. Pizzeria Uno asks you to move back in time to the '40s and '50s when Italian food was really Italian and prepared by doting "momma mias" and served by concerned waiters with black bow ties and white towels over their arms. The colors, the lights, even the seats and benches are remembrances of things past.

Curtain going up on Grills and Groovy Places.

Brandy-Ho
San Francisco, CA

BRANDY-HO

San Francisco, CA

Brandy-Ho is located on Broadway in a three story building which combines aspects of Chinese and Italian cultures — which also exist on the neon illuminated street in San Francisco. Italian neo classicism is blended with the Chinese "craftsman" style found in the palaces of Beijing's Forbidden City and both employ "highly ordered structural systems in which structure becomes building ornament." On the facade neon is very evident as are the brilliant red beams and columns painted with auto body paint to simulate the shine of red lacquer added on to the neo-classic facade of the building. The columns have neon and glass capitals and similar columns appear in the two story high, 23' tall foyer. Red neon handrails lead up to the second floor dining and banquet rooms. Beyond the foyer the structural elements "define a series of discrete spaces each with its own unique character."

The spacial progression is marked off by red square columns that stand to either side of the black granite central aisle and the "display kitchen" appears here as a brightly lit stage; it is viewed from a raised dining platform. Over the kitchen opening an abstract Chinese roof cave is capped by acrylic tubes lit by concealed green neon, and these rings become the traditional green roof tiles. At the end of the central axis, in the rear dining room, a massive rock cliff is revealed through windows and skylights.

The color scheme is simple; red lacquer, black enamel and white with additional touches of green and greenery. The excellent lighting plan lets it all happen.

Design: Goldman Architects, San Francisco, CA
Principal: John Goldman, AIA
Photographer: Jane Lidz

WOKMAN

Mission Viejo, CA

Since this completely contemporary design was created for Michael and Ann Chiang, white and blue (the death colors for traditional Chinese) were omitted from the color scheme which otherwise seems to sing out with every other color to be found in a Crayola crayon box. The primary finishes in this unique setting of 3000 sq. ft. are red, yellow, purple, teal and black ceramic tiles and laminates and the fun feature is the red enameled wok, sliced in half, used as wall sconces. The tile stripes, made up in varigated rainbow bands run across the floor — up the walls — and around columns. The space is alive with curves; radiused soffits and inverted ceiling rings banded in neon complement the round tables, curving banquettes and the overscaled

rotating fortune cookie which displays amusing changing messages. Even the glass block wall takes its turn.

The main food presentation counter and center of activity is covered in white tile striped with bands of the colored tiles. Behind the wall is paved with red tiles that continue the "good luck" color that also appears on the ceiling fans hanging from the vaulted purple ceiling and on the red metal and wire grid dividers around the seating in the 84 seat restaurant. The Wokman's logo appears over the service area and it is echoed in the mirrored wall adjacent to it.

Design: R.W. Smith and Co., Costa Mesa, CA
   Patty Webb
Photographer: Susan Seitz, Huntington Beach, CA

CALIFORNIA BEACH ROCK 'N' SUSHI

Los Angeles, CA

Kazu Miyama, the owner of two other Rock 'N' Sushi restaurants wanted a real blast — a show-stopper — for his new dining place on Melrose Ave. which is hardly the place for quiet restraint. The architect, Ted Tokio Tanaka, who is noted for his "cool restraint and minimalist influenced projects" was invited to turn the 4000 sq. ft. dining room and 1500 sq. ft. of terrace into a center of theatrical excitement — and that he did!

A neon billboard sign — brilliant in color — up on the second level of the facade brightens the exterior on Melrose Ave. which is already ablaze with color and light. The low ceilinged interior is filled with stylized triangular forms representing waves, abstract constructions, platforms and connecting ramps — all placed at angles "to set the room in motion." The restaurant is vivid with color; bright blue, aquas and greens, slashes of purple, magenta and red. The beachcomber mural helps set the scene and the mood as does the "stage-set" just opposite the outdoor terrace which is piled up with sand, supports a lifeguard station, surfboard inflatable sharks and more wonderful and colorful murals.

Behind the blue, black and neon outlined sushi bar bubbling waters dance up and down in illuminated tubes in time to the rock beat of the music videos that are evident everywhere in the room. Since Rock 'N' Sushi is a theatrical experience it did take every theatrical and clever device to light the space and fill it with the California Beach spirit.

Design: Ted Tokio Tanaka, Venica, CA
Murals: Doug Kanegawa
Photographer: Tom Bonner, Venice, CA

CHOPSTICKS

Pasadena, CA

Chopsticks is a contemporary Chinese cafe concept that features a "grazing" menu of inexpensive Chinese/Thai dishes prepared with a distinctive California slant. All the stir-fry dishes, salads, dim sum which dominate the health-oriented, MSG-free, menu are prepared in the open kitchen which, in turn, dominates the design of the enclosed operation which takes up 2500 sq. ft. A cement arch is the entrance into the open patio where diners can sit out and enjoy the passing parade of Pasadenians — under trees alive with light. Inside the multi-angled bar is faced with turquoise ceramic tiles and the high bar stools are made of natural oak with turquoise seat pads. Some stools face the un-ending show of food preparation and decoration going on in the clean and efficient stainless-steel kitchen behind the counter while those set around the tall communal tables have a high-perched look at the same action. Off-white quarry tiles are laid on the floor and the oak bordered tables are covered with a creamy laminate.

The lighting plan combines low voltage tungsten lamps on decorative brass tracks with recessed incandescents and bands of neon that light up the gridded ceiling. A nice touch — and worth seeking out — is the enclosed bubbling salt water fish tanks that stick out of the wall in the rest room.

PANE E VINO

Montecito, Santa Barbara, CA

The Santa Barbara "in crowd" has discovered Pane e Vino which was formerly the Buell House. Chef Claudio Marcheson and his partner Pietro Bernardi combine talent and flair with the authentic regional Italian cuisine that has made this the place to be seen — eating. In addition, getting top billing and co-starring with the food is the "warm, charming and intimate" ambience created by Gina Muzingo.

The large white squares of quarry tiles on the floor are accented and bordered with smaller squares of green tile. The restaurant also boasts of a deli-take-out section that is designed with dark wood cases, cabinets and shelves with matching moldings and wainscotting that wrap around the provincial setting. One of the local publications, reviewing the restaurant, said, "I love the decor. If I were redoing my kitchen I'd send the designer over to Pane e Vino to see the warm gleaming wood, the green and black marble, and white and green floor. I wouldn't mind the cases filled with cheeses, salamis, and antipasto either or the shelves lined with bottles of straw wrapped chianti and imported Italian foods. The Italians can make a can of tomatoes look like a work of art." (Hilary Dole Klein)

Design: Muzingo Associates, Los Angeles, CA
Principal: Gina Muzingo

KNOWLWOOD'S

Santa Ana, CA

The Knowlwood fast food restaurants are a "culinary homage to a bygone era" — a tribute to what life and food was like back in the 40s and 50s. On these pages and the following ones, we show two of the award winning designs created by the team of Steve Eisenman, Geoff Beckham and Gary Selufsky. From the outside this restaurant combines Streamline Moderne with echos of art deco but the canteen looks like a corrugated metal garage, circa 1940. The Canteen fulfills on the inside what it promised on the outside; it does resemble a clean garage or firehouse set up for a party. The area is filled with authentic period pieces picked up at rummage sales and garage sales and many are from the chain's owner's own collection of memorabilia. Old stamped advertising signs, license plates of the right vintage, tires and such mingle with full size telegraph poles and what isn't "authentic" is authentically reproduced like the cast-iron manhole covers set into the floor in front of the "road side hamburger stand" that provides the food and visual entertainment for the hungry. The chain's motto is inscribed on the manhole cover, — "Knowlwood — Home of the World's Best Hamburger."

The telegraph poles carry the downlights in the dining area where the tables are covered with red "oilcloth" and the booths are upholstered with mottled red vinyl. The amusing murals pick up where the dimensional poles leave off and go on and on into the distance.

Design: Beckham & Eisenman, Irvine, CA
Photographer: Milroy/McAleer, Newport Beach, CA

KNOWLWOOD

Irvine, CA

It ain't fancy — but IT IS fun. An old, worn-out 40s pick-up truck gets a new lease on a different style of life inside the hangar-like structure that houses this Knowlwood's operation. The truck has been turned into a sit-down counter for the fast food diners with "antique" chrome-and-vinyl pull-up stools around it. The "back-of-the-truck" is loaded with boxes and cartons wearing labels and logos of another era. The interior architecture is almost completely lost under a coat of charcoal gray paint but the old gym lights with their wire masks hang down to light up the things worth seeing like the splendid period juke

box. Here the floor is finished in wood and the tables are stained dark mahogany complemented with white laminate tops. The yellow of the truck/counter is repeated on the vinyl upholstery of the booths where it is teamed up with royal blue. The order counter and the open kitchen beyond are flavored with motifs and elements found in diners of the 40s; white enameled surfaces banded with strips of chrome, cornice caps of stainless steel, and neon. Neon lines also zig zag their way through the dim upper reaches of the space defining the areas and activities below.

Design: Beckham & Eisenman, Irvine, CA
Photographer: Milroy/McAleer, Newport Beach, CA

CUCINA! CUCINA!

Chandler's Cove, Seattle, WA

Cucina is Italian for kitchen and Kitchen Kitchen is what Cucina Cucina is all about. It is alive — it throbs with fresh excitement and so much of that splutter and sparkle eminates from the open display kitchen aglitter in stainless steel and bright yellow tiles that complement the rest of the color scheme which clashes a hot red tinged with pink against a brilliant teal — a sort of take-off on the Italian national colors. The woody interior contributes to the friendly, informal attitude of this dining room that can seat 166 patrons and another 110 with lounge seats — all with a marvelous view of Lake Union viewed through the floor to ceiling windows. The bar, off the entry is finished in knotty pine accented with stainless steel and verdigris copper. The central dining space is raised and surrounded by teal columns and a psychedelic painted ceiling running to riot in yellow, teal and the hot red/pink caps the central area. The black concrete floors are spattered and accented with terra cotta tiles and the floors go with the black steel cafe chairs as well as with the wicker chairs.

Cucina! Cucina! is friendly — it's informal — and the exposed duct work — the very visible and utilitarian kitchen — the can of extra virgin olive oil set out on each table — the bright colors and modern art posters all combine to create an ambience that invites the diner to return — even if only to go to the rest room to check out the recorded conversation — in Italian that takes the place of the canned music.

Design: Mesher, Shing Associates, Seattle, WA

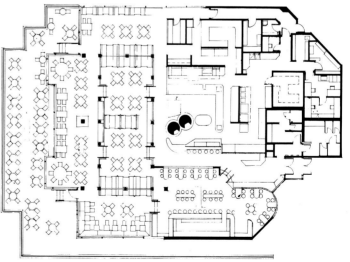

PAPPAS GRILL

Toronto, Ont., Canada

Pappas grill, says the architect/designer is an "architecturally clean, simple space with elements of Greek and French Mediterranean influences" and the 5734 sq. ft. space was designed to attract and keep the neighborhood clientele as well as the tourists who come to Danforth St.

The three level restaurant seats 168 patrons and the upper level is the open kitchen encircled by glass cases filled with meats, salads and pastries. A rustic clay oven appears at the entrance to Pappas. It is showmanship; "it attracts and draws your gaze back through the open three levels of the restaurant" that is textured with brick, tiles, wood and stucco.

Design: Hirschberg Design Group, Toronto, Ont., Canada
Principal: Martin Hirschberg
Photographer: Frazer Day

COCONUT GRILL

Thornhill, Ont., Canada

The patron steps through and under a Victorian trellised walkway leaving the noisiest street behind and entering into a romantic, tropic island of greenery, canvas umbrellas, whirring ceiling fans hanging from a corrugated ceiling with service pipes and ductwork scurrying across it. The 120 seat restaurant is located on a 6700 sq. ft. corner plot in a shopping plaza. During the daylight hours light pours into this idyllic setting from the windows on two sides.

The kitchen is open for viewing and the latticed hurricane shutters are pulled up so that the show can be enjoyed by everyone. The louvers are backlit to suggest sunlight filtering through. The traffic pattern is indicated by brick pavers on the floor and areas are marked off with flooring, railings and posts of gray weathered timber. The colors are cool and fresh; lots of aqua, green and white, the soft weathered gray, and splashes of bright color comes from the Caribbean landscape painted on one wall. Stuffed birds sit on railings and trellises adding their bright blobs of color.

*The semi-circular counter/bar swings about in view of the kitchen and the dining table fan out from there.

Design: Hirschberg Design Group, Toronto, Ont., Canada
Principal: Martin Hirschberg
Photographer: Frazer Day

PIZZA STRADA

Raleigh/Durham & Memphis International Airports

"Influences of the 1950s contemporary style converge with attitudes and elements of today in this quick serve restaurant/bar." To create a screen effect, classic column fragments and details are applied to the mirrored wall. Accent walls are sheathed in a figured mahogany veneer and an overlay of black wood grids becomes a strong patterned background for the dining and bar areas. A gloss black wall divides the two.

For the Durham/Raleigh operation, ebony stained chair frames are upholstered with black leather and molded plastic chairs pull up to the granite topped tables. Tomato red and forest green striped awning fabric is used to upholster the banquette seating.

Both airport settings share the black and white mosaic tile floor and the checkered pattern that is used to modify and identify elements and areas in both. In the Memphis Airport's Pizza Strada an overscaled mahogany cornice and a band of rich forest green and white tile serve to attract the travelers out on the concourse. A fully exposed pizza kitchen gets an eye-filling place in the plan and the wrap around checkerboard pattern emphasizes the location. A black background menu board pops out the rear lit photographs of prepared foods and the open-to-view displays provide extra stimuli for the tired or just bored traveler. Light gray granite tabletops contrast with the tile, and mirrors, mahogany trim, the deep cordovan painted paneling and the forest green accents.

Design: DiLeonardo International, Warwick, RI
Photographer: Warren Jagger

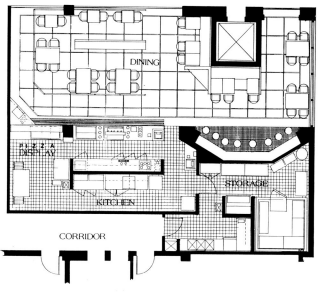

PIZZERIA UNO

Massapequa, NY

There is a sense of deja vu when the diner steps into one of the
Pizzeria Uno restaurants. The 40s are revived and much of the
nostalgia comes from the use of black and white tiles on the walls
and the black and white checkered tablecloths on the tables
standing out on the natural wood stained floors. Ebonized
chairs with off-white or peach upholstered seats surround the
tables. Four seater booths are separated by mahogany slatted
partitions and corrugated glass dividers. The high-tech, hangar
ceiling of corrugated metal and service pipes and ducts is gridded
off with electrified tracks from which hang metal dome shades
over tables and booths. The tracks also carry spots and floods to
warm up the ambience as well as the old-fashioned ceiling fans
that make their contribution to the retro look.

The open kitchen and service area is outlined by the dark green
wainscotting and mahogany topped counter under the red and
blue neon enriched fascia. The long mahogany bar is illuminated
by milk glass pendant globes and the "period-style" chromed
bar stools are upholstered in maroon and black like the chan-
neled backs of the banquettes.

Outside, the facade is painted a deep green color and the black
signage band is appliqued with old fashioned gold leaf raised letters. Floor to ceiling windows provide an unobstructed look into
the restaurant with its flashes of neon signage.

Design: Tony Chi/Albert Chen, NY
Photographer: Dub Rogers

SPECIALTY STORES

We are living in the era of Specialization. In fashion retailing the successful retailers are those who have found a niche — a special or particular customer in the market and found a way to satisfy her needs and a way of catering to her image of herself in a setting that complements her — and the product. Food specialty stores are specialty stores because they too are satisfying in depth the cravings and satiating the appetites of a special group of the buying society. It is not "something for everyone" but "everything for someone."

A cheese store, to succeed today, can't just carry a few traditional types, names or brands but it has to catalogue an encyclopedia of cheeses; from all corners of the world — from cows, goat, sheep or exotic animals' milk, and to satisfy the dietary requirements of the health-conscious, yuppified society. The store must inventory low fat, low cholesterol and low sodium cheeses of infinite varieties and degrees of spreadability along with the rich, fat and fullsome flavored cheeses that gourmets expect. "Damn the cholesterol — full fat ahead!" What would cheese be without the right crackers, wafers, biscuits, bread? Just as the fashion specialty store carries the accessories necessary to complete the outfit, so does the food specialty store set aside counter and/or shelf space for the accoutrements that complete the snack, the hors d'oeuvre, the picnic or the feast. Tea and coffee shops will not only contain the variety of beans in bags and blends in boxes but will also carry the teapots and coffeemakers, the brewing aids and coffee filters, the cups, cozies and cannisters to make the selection complete. Since diversified blends and brews are so in demand that they are now promoted as gift items and the made-to-order-gift packaging has become an integral part of the product and service one finds in coffee and tea shops. How can one buy what one has only sniffed — but not tasted? The specialty coffee and tea shops now is often a cafe in miniature where the prospective client can sip the blend of the day — caffeinated or decaffeinated.

In this chapter we are showing some of the ways these specialty stores are attracting and satisfying their customers. Rather than feature the "staples," we are highlighting the egocentric specialties: wine, candy, cookies, coffee and tea — and water. The Watermark shop is devoted wholly and solely to the sale of water and that is about as specialized as it gets! The new look of Hickory Farms best explains how diversified — yet focalized — the specialty store can be. Our wine and liquor stores are as elegant and refined as the Wine Reserve in Philadelphia or like the Esprit du Vin, in London, they can be a trip down to the wine cellars of another time. In Panache and Bergin's the wine bar plays an important part in promoting and selling the wines while Expresso Liquor adds a continental look that elevates the shopping experience into the adventure of taste — and tasting. To see it is to want it and the sweets lovers see "it" in Sweet Things and Sweet Factory — and they buy it. In these two shops the candy becomes the color, the texture and the decor of the selling spaces. At Fanny Farmer's the "old fashioned, good old days" setting makes the chocolates appear as delectable as we "remember" them from our childhood.

Warm and woody, steely sleek and sophisticated, crisp clean and clinical, — each type of setting calls out to a different kind of customer; a shopper with a unique self image looking for something in a setting that is right for her or him. That is what specialization is all about; giving the customer what she wants — where she wants it — and in a way that pleases as many of her senses as possible.

Classic Cookie
Woodbridge Mall
Woodbridge, NJ

THE COFFEE BEANERY

Flushing, MI

The desire for whole coffee beans and specialty blends is becoming one of the trademarks of the affluent, upscaled young consumers and the Coffee Beanery, headquartered in Flushing, MI is becoming one of the Meccas for the faithful. The 13-year-old chain now has over 25 mall outlets for their variety of more than 50 kinds of coffee beans and full line of related items. "We're satisfying the public's appetite for great tasting coffee to complement its irresistible aroma and at the same time we've created an atmosphere where customers feel comfortable in a warm and friendly setting," says JoAnn Shaw, president of the company.

The exterior facade contemporary; natural woods accented with strips of black marble and banded with an illuminated brass signage strip. The same horizontal layered look of tiers of oak and cherrywood over tiers of the same continues inside where the gleaming silver roaster dominates atop the serving counter. Acrylic gravity feed cannisters are neatly lined up on successive shelves filled with an assortment of brass labeled coffee beans while other shelves are used for the display of coffee makers, prepared coffees and the complements. Cabinets are topped

with shadow boxes for special featured displays. The off-white vinyl floor echoes the creamy laminate used for the tops and edges of the shelves and the counter top.

Stores vary from about 300 sq. ft. up to 1500 sq. ft. with the average shop being about 800 sq. ft.

Design: Hunter Five Architects, Southfield, MI
Visual Merchandising Consultant: Marc Bear

GEORGETOWN COFFEE & TEA

Washington, DC

In elegant, historic and trendy-new Georgetown is this small crowded, cramped and odoriferous shop where for over 30 years the knowing have come for the unusual selection of gourmet coffee beans, bulk and packaged teas and all the related items that go with making and enjoying a fine cup of coffee or tea — and the space looks as though it was always just like it is now. The tunnel-like store is 16' wide by 50' long and it is bright with spots but the well target lamps do not wipe out the shadows and textures and the faded colors that give the shop an almost Dickensian quality. Four years ago the shop was taken over by Milan-born Luciana Caleb and she now personally oversees the personal selections from the many burlap bags stacked up, and raised up at the rear end of the store. The blackboard above lists the specials and the featured blends but it does fight for prominence against the other signs that fill the store. The teas are politely and properly lined up, on sagging shelves, in glass display cannisters. Prepared packages and a selection of cups, mugs, teapots and such are also set out for viewing. The floors are wood, aged and worn as are the shelves lined up high along the unobstrusive gray walls. For those who can't wait there are always a few pots of fresh coffee brewing — if you don't object to styro cups.

Photographer: Father & Suns

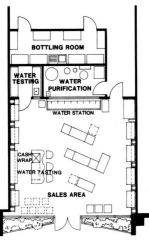

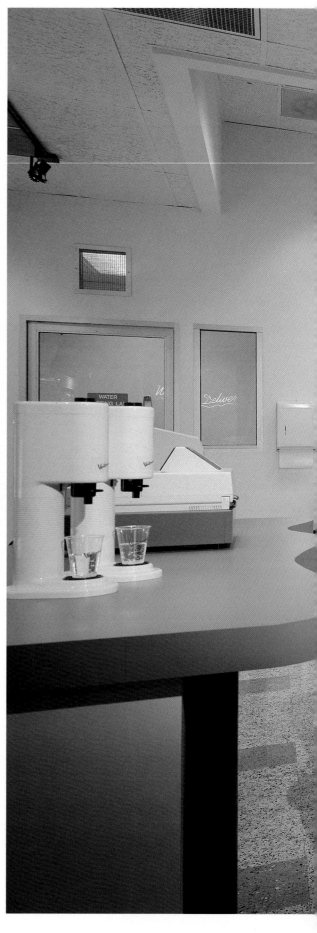

WATERMARK

Walnut Creek, CA

The Watermark store "addresses all segments of the water market under one roof" Here is offered bottled water, a retail line of flavored spring waters, bulk water fill-up, home and office delivery, water dispensing systems for commercial and office use and more. Each center is also a licensed plant where water can be purified, dispensed and bottled fresh daily.

The center has "a casual, inviting atmosphere with a crisp, clean, cheerful and professional but not intimidating ambience." The graphic design elements designed by Cole Martinez Curtis are incorporated into the store with the sky blue ceiling. "The purple mountains majesty are painted on the walls and the yellow valance is really the sun rising over the mountains." There is lots of white juxtaposed with the yellow and blue graphics which are found on the free standing fixtures, and the cash/wrap counter top. A large Watermark logo appears over the water bar on the back wall. The color scheme is repeated "in the blue neon waveline dancing across the store front windows and highlighting other white neon signs.

Design: Cole, Martinez Curtis, Marina del Rey, CA
Partners in Charge: Leo Martinez/Jill Cole
Project Executive: Peter De Caro
Photographer: Toshi Yoshimica

THE WINE RESERVE

Rittenhouse Sq., Philadelphia, PA

The bottles had to speak for themselves. "The simple white rectangular space has an almost monastic quality which encourages contemplation of the wines." To facilitate that contemplation Hugh Boyd designed utilitarian wooden racks to contain the bottles and each one is individually cradled to insure proper airflow and temperature. "The detailing of the mahogany and red-bronze racks was intended to be especially transparent so that the maximum amount of each bottle's surface could be exposed" and the color of the wood stain was selected to best conceal any staining that might result from breakage. The quartzite stone floor was selected for its color and the fact that it is impervious to wine stains since the gray stone is varied with streaks of rust and bands of speckled mica.

The lighting of the space is generally either recessed or concealed so as not to distract from the contemporary wine cellar atmosphere though some spots are used to highlight the displays.

Design: Boyd Associates, Montclair, NJ
Principal: Hugh A. Boyd, AIA
Photographer: Durston Saylor

IRVINE FARMERS MARKET

Horton Plaza, San Diego, CA

Though part of the market shown on pages 28 and 29, the Wine Cellar is set off in an alcove almost like a free-standing operation. It has a facade made up of lattice work formed of mahogany stained lath strips and the central arched opening rests upon a pair of channelated pilasters. Inside, the ceiling is painted black and from it extend rows of incandescents targeted at the mahogany colored shelves that cover the three walls of the space. The floor is also laid with wood and in the middle of the floor is a display featuring wines nestled in old wine vats and stacked up on bleached wood crates that they are delivered in. More of these light wood crates and cartons create an interesting border design atop the dark wood shelf units.

Design: Beckham & Eisenman, Irvine, CA
Photographer: Milroy/McAleer, Newport Beach, CA

EXPRESSO LIQUOR

Crossroads S/C, Orlando, FL

The Expresso Liquor store is located in the new Disney Crossroads shopping center and the space is about 2500 sq. ft. The designers have employed a simple but functional plan for this store. In the center is a round (actually octagonal) wine tasting bar that also serves as a cashier station. From that central point the surrounding display shelves are angled so that the clerk has 100% visibility down each aisle for security control and customer service — with minimal walking distances required.

The color scheme is geared towards creating a "contemporary,

old-world, Italian style look." The floor is checkerboarded in garnet and gray vinyl tiles around the garnet and gray laminated central counter. The surrounding radiating low wine racks are finished in mahogany and trimmed with black. They sit on a wine colored carpet. The overhead canvas signage also radiates out from the octagonal superstructure rich in dripping green foliage. The signs identify the areas and types of wines to be found beneath them. Incandescent, on the spoked ceiling, "warm up" the bottles angled for show.

Design: Forum Architecture, Maitland, FL

PANACHE

Fullerton, CA

The "Wine and Spiritorium" is found at the far end of the upscaled Panache market, gourmet-to-go, restaurant/cafe (see pages 18-19). The white bistro tables and chairs are set out on the black and white checkered floor — some are under European styled white canvas umbrellas. Under the neon signage on the white wall is a compact gray/white marble wine bar and counter. The high stools are lacquered black. Wines for tasting are lined up behind the counter and wines-to-go are arranged in soldier-like fashion on the tall white laminate cubicled partitions. At the very farthest end, under a dramatic series of white build up blocks, is a refrigerator with chilled wines and champagnes. Green plants and the blue sky ceiling suggest an outdoor cafe setting and the recessed lights keep the area visible but still romantic.

Design: Bolton Design Group, Carmel Valley, CA

ESPRIT DU VIN

Wimbledon, England

This is the second generation Esprit du Vin shop designed by Fitch & Co. The task facing the design team led by Mark Landini was to "develop a modern interior with traditional references which recapture the atmosphere of an authentic wine trading outlet."

The designers have come up with a core design theme that is "charismatic, witty and sensual." On the ground floor the walls are surfaced in sand and cement and the plaster ceiling has been tinted with a vibrant blue wash finish to "provide an exciting visual contrast and fresh backdrop to the elaborate racking system." The racking is sculpted in a variety of metal finishes and constructed to allow the wine to be stored horizontally. Sample bottles are angled forward towards the shoppers to provide access to the information on the label.

A dome light made of steel and black metal is suspended over the main sales area where "it dominates the central space rather like a spider throwing light around the perimeter and illuminating the racks and the merchandise."

A walk-in cooler constructed on sheet metal and lined with old industrial "fridge" shelving is located in the rear of the shop. Downstairs, in an atmosphere like a traditional wine cellar, customers can sample wines and transact business. A beaten

parquet floor, timber beams, bare bricks and remnants of old newspapers "capture the essence of an antiquated cellar filled with maturing vintages."

Design: Fitch & Co., London, England

BERGIN'S WINE BAR

South St. Seaport, New York, NY

Bergin's Wine Bar is a wine bar in its truest sense though it also sells "spirits-to-go." The area is a custom designed, walk-in box complete with windows which enable sippers-to-be to see the wine cooling and the beer kegs ready for tapping. Seven brass "beer towers" proclaim the different types of beer available at Bergin's. Ice bins are set into the counter display areas and chilling wines, cold beers and snacking cheeses are presented.

The focal point of the wine bar is the undulating bar of mahogany veneer topped with white corian. The floor is laid with natural terra cotta tiles outlined with white grout and overhead, on a track system, are sharp and vital low voltage tungsten lamps that bring out the color of the wood walls and the bottles on the display shelves.

Design: Martin Dorf Associates, NY

147

SWEET THINGS

Claypool Center, Indianapolis, IN

The mall entrance to the 540 sq. ft. Sweet Things is white tile gridded in strawberry red and wrapped with bands of assorted color neons. The tiles on the floor are also small squares of white interrupted with patterns of the deep rose/red tiles that create a moving traffic line into the shop. To the left of the entrance are floor to ceiling lucite tubes — like organ pipes — that were designed by the architect to hold and dispense the assorted colors and flavors of jelly beans. For extra visual impact the tubes are banded in neon. "Since neon light is the unifying element, it acts as an interest point," says Joseph Ballinger.

Inside, a hot red/pink and white grid wallpaper wraps around some of the wall areas and gray enameled columns with square caps and bases are used as decorative architectural elements. Canvas awnings, to match, are suspended over the glass shelves that hold gift ideas. "We wanted to create a spacial relationship

with light and draw people into the store. Candy is a tiny item so it was a challenge to enlarge the overall product by using the color scheme provided."

Design: Ballinger Design Associates, Indianapolis, IN
Principal: G. Joseph Ballinger, AIA
Photographer: Ballinger/Chilluffo

FANNY FARMER

Town City Center, Cleveland, OH

The nation's largest candy retailer changed its store design and corporate image to reflect the company's turn-of-the-century roots. This store is designed to look like the traditional American candy store with an interior that blends woods, brass, marble and ceramic tiles. This "warm, old-world mood is a departure from the sleek, contemporary interiors of the Fanny Farmer shops of the '80s." Traditional millwork and moldings are used on the cabinets, shelves and cornices of the stocking units built around the space and the free standing counter that cuts across the plan, cater-corner, is also made of wood with large glass enclosed areas above. Pendant bowls of milk glass rimmed with brass serve as decorative ceiling fixtures while other incandescents are recessed in the ceiling over the packaged items.

The familiar cameo face returns to the portrait face first used in the 1950s. "The old cameo is a more classic, ageless portrait and to complement it the packaging colors are being changed to vanilla creme and chocolate brown."

Arch: Larson Architects, Lakewood, OH
Principal: Jim Larson
Photographer: Mickey Jones, University Heights, OH

ED & DON'S

Ala Moana S/C, Honolulu, HI

In an open space located on the lower level of the giant and still growing Ala Moana Mall is this handsome independent candy and gift shop designed to attract the locals as well as the tourists who flock here. The floor is paved with large squares of white tile and the walls are finished in warm-white. Mulberry laminates sheath the circular display platforms and the self-illuminated, glass topped chocolate counter that angles across the rear of the store. The walls on the right are saw-toothed in plan; each bay is angled and set back from the one in front so that the shoppers on the concourse get to see the merchandise face on as they walk by. Each bay is capped with a deep il-luminated cornice and the whole small area is bright with light. Fluorescent ceiling fixtures are abetted by tracks of in-candescents. Neon swirls over the rear counter identify it as the Chocolate Boutique. On the white platforms, up front, are gift cartons and containers of local candies and nut and chocolate products ready to travel home with the travelers.

Photographer: Father & Suns

SWEET FACTORY

England

Sweet Factory represents an entirely new way to retail confectionery in England. Operating on "self-select" principles, it offers the shopper a fun and exciting way to buy sweets in a color-filled environment where what you see is what you want to buy — and you buy it because it is displayed under brilliant light. It is like a space trip to Candyland in the 21st century with interplanetary light fixtures filling the ceiling area with futuristic design and the lucite dispensers are lined up in a space odyssey laboratory. An on-the-floor robot is there to assist, to inform, and to add to the next century ambience.

The customers are invited to fill up the generous size bags provided for use with the easy-to-use dispensers. "The colour-coordinated confectionery, which is sourced from all over the world, is shown off to maximum advantage in the purpose designed merchandise units — aided by mirror reflections they present a seemingly endless array of products."

Design: Michael Peters Group, London, England

BLOOMS BAKERY-TO-GO

Quality Inn, Beachwood, OH

What won't they think of next? A bakery in a hotel lobby? Why not? Just off the main lobby, sending out olefactory signals, is this mini-bakery/to-go operation with black and brass cases to show off the breads, rolls, muffins, pastries and cakes. Touched with nostalgia and a provincial attitude, the tiled walls recall "gemutlische" bakeries and coffee houses in old Vienna. Even the mirrored arched "window" with black mullions adds to that look along with the artifacts and "antiques" lined up on the shelf over the orange and blue tiled border. Behind the glass cases and facing the traffic aisle is a complete, mini-working kitchen where they can whip up, pack up and send off the provisions. To enhance the cozy, comfortable area, greenery and flowering plants abound.

Design: Babcock & Schmidt, Bath, OH

153

HICKORY FARMS

Gwinette Place Mall, Atlanta, GA

Hickory Farms is a national retailer of specialty foods with over 300 stores in a wide range of markets, malls and retail centers. The stores usually average between 1200 to 4000 sq. ft.

The retailers approached SDI because they wanted "a more upscaled prototype store concept as well as better merchandising techniques, fixturing, packaging and point-of-sale and in-store communication materials." SDI came up with a smaller but very modular store concept with a flexible plan to accommodate the changing seasonal requirements — laid out on a diagonal scheme. They also developed "signature" furniture pieces which are based on traditional hutches and tables but they also feature non-traditional colors and patterns for a "folk charm." A nationally known photographer and a food stylist contributed to the point-of-sale graphic program. The traditional large store opening remains so that the customer can "see the breadth of what the store has to offer." Daniel Conetta, V.P. of Marketing for Hickory Farms said, "Food has become fashion and it must have appetite appeal when presented in a store as it would in the home. Our new design, therefore, replicates the primary usage of our products."

Design: Space Design International, Cincinnati, OH
Principal: John Heatherman

FAST FOODS

Time was when Fast Foods was synonymous with frankfurters and hamburgers and the big decision was whether or not to put cheese or relish on the burger or opt for mustard and/or sauerkraut on the frank. When it came to side orders it was french fries — with or without ketchup. I am oversimplifying, but Fast Foods today are gastronomic world tours or around-the-world in 80 bites!

Walk into almost any food court in a modest mall or in a super spectacular shopping center and you are greeted with sights and smells that only a few years ago was reserved for first class voyagers. Mixed in with the traditional, all American hamburgers and franks are Chinese egg-rolls and egg foo young, Italian pizzas and more than just pepperoni pies, Greek kabobs and souvlakis, Indian curries on cardboard plates, Japanese sushi, sushimi and sometimes soba, and Israeli falafel, hummus, taboli and pita packed sandwiches. From the French we got croissants, filled croissants and croissant filled sandwiches (an American improvement). Mexican morsels have gone way beyond tacos and tortillas and now we have "healthy" Mexican munching.

Health and health-oriented fast foods have swept the courts and concessions are spilling over with salads, garden-fresh vegetables, and fresh fruit concoctions. Yogurt has moved up from the dessert end of the menu into main course entrees. Low fat, low cholesterol and low sodium items get special attention and are featured on signs. Potato specialties — fries, skins or stuffed — are satisfying the new breed of fast food mavens — and the signs often say "fried in vegetable oils." Chicken used to be a dinner food, now it is out there as breasts in sandwiches, as thighs coated and fried, as wings treated Buffalo-style and in bits and pieces called nuggets or fingers to be dipped in a variety of sauces.

Fast foods today are soup, salads, spuds and sandwiches — international specialties, treats to the palette and finger-lickin' good — and good for you. Ice cream, like yogurt, is a meal in cup or a dessert on a come and the option of toppings is endless. It can be "rich" — it can be "diet" or "non-fat" — it can be "pure cream"; the decision is up to the diner. Our selections attempt to cover the range of foods. Many of our examples are to be found in malls — in food courts — while others exist as free-standing operations alone and apart from other food concessions.

McDonald's is an excellent example of what has developed in Fast Foods. It is upscaled and upgraded with a more varied menu and with store designs that are compatible with their more upwardly mobile patrons. It reflects the taste level of the office workers and the junior and not-so-junior executives that come here because it is convenient, comfortable, fast and relatively inexpensive. Le Croissant and Au Bon Pan are excellent examples of the French cafe style adapted to fast foods. Though some are located in up-scaled malls as many or more are to be found in midtown and downtown locations catering to a business-oriented clientele who still wants fast service but with a degree of style and taste — and variety. Macheesmo Mouse is fun — it's different and it is targeted at the diet-conscious individual who wants more than a bland salad or a fat-free yogurt for lunch. Taco Bell, the nationwide chain, brings popular versions of Mexican foods to the great middle-American public in pleasant and appealing surroundings. Pickle, Pepper and Romaine is smart and simple just as its menu is light, nutritious and delicious. It is designed for and caters to a sophisticated shopper in a downtown spot and it wears the tradition of the structure in which it is housed with stylish insouciance. There are several examples of ice cream/yogurt operations and we hope the viewer will appreciate the infinite variety of styles, colors and materials used in the presentation of these ever-popular products.

Fast foods are fun and there is something for everyone out there no matter what the preference or dietary needs. The foods are prepared and presented in bright, colorful and stimulating settings where time flies, foods are served and eaten quickly if not in haste and the turn over is rarely a problem.

Michele's Waffles
New York, NY

McDONALDS

3 Nationwide Place, Columbus, OH

The 6500 sq. ft. fast food operation is unique in several ways. It serves as the chain's Midwest flagship store and it is also situated in a six story atrium of a Columbus corporation building. The designers had to create a restaurant that would serve inexpensive food "yet display aesthetic qualities similar to the high quality of the development."

The restaurant is designed to suit the office workers who come here so the materials are more sophisticated and of higher quality than one would associate with "fast-foods." Granite and slate were used on the floors and marble on the walls along with original artwork. Draperies are applied to the windows and generally a warmer, darker and "quieter" color scheme and lighting plan was selected to contrast with the bright fluorescent offices the patrons have escaped from. Wood, cloth seatbacks, Roman shades, incandescents on dimmers, pendant fixtures with a glowing red accent and all the original artwork "soften the space" and upscale it at the same time. Bright canopies with a copper patina finish serves as focal points over the serving counters and provide the interim step between the sharply illuminated food preparation area and the dimly-lit and relaxing dining area.

Design: Bohm-NBBJ, Columbus, OH
Principal-in-Charge: Myron A. Pettit
Principal: Design: James H. Schurtzinger, AIA
Photographer: Artog/D.G. Olshowsky

AMERICAN HAMBURGER

Independence Mall, Kingston, MA

The facade of American Hamburger simulates, in line and spirit, a compact diner of the 50s. The designers attempted to side-step the cliche format used in most fast-food stands and they brought the actual preparation kitchen up into the front-of-the-house design. The open flame broiling — the strong selling point for the hamburger company — sizzles into sight "while preserving the integrity of depth of space."

The patron steps up to the silvery counter covered with Armore textured metal and a triple archway, over it, like a rainbow arc of chromed metal trimmed with red and blue neon signage. The actual kitchen area is sheathed in a metallic formica and capped with a wave like fascia outlined in chrome and row after row of red and blue neon streamers. Glass blocks and ceramic floor tiles reaffirm the 50s look while up in the ceiling myriad pinpoint downlights illuminate the glittery area below; "a little old-fashioned diner flair" according to Tony Chi, the designer.

Design: Tony Chi/Albert Chen, Architects, NY
Photographer: Dub Rogers, W.H. Rogers III, NY

LE DRUG — EDITO-RESTO

Montreal, Que.

The Parisian-inspired Drug-Store combines two fast food concessions with seating for 78 and an international magazine shop. The 5000 sq. ft. basement space was "meticulously crafted with a long lasting look — something that could become an institution on Luarier St." — one of the trendy new shopping streets in fashionable Montreal. A glass wall encased in a large red lacquered grill was designed as a "transparent" space separator between the magazine shop and the fast food concessions so that all the diners can have an unobstructed view across the glazing. A continuous signage band conceals the indirect fluorescents along the perimeter wall and also gives the illusion of a higher ceiling. Red neon ribbons activate the ceiling.

The floor is laid and patterned with black and white tiles and a checkerboard design of black and white trims columns, wainscots the walls and borders the floors next to the gray and white marble counters. The counters are edged with rows of stainless steel railing upon which the trays glide along. Bright red reappears on a focal red column and on the enameled bistro chairs.

Design: Camdi International, Montreal, Que.
Project Manager: Patty Xenos

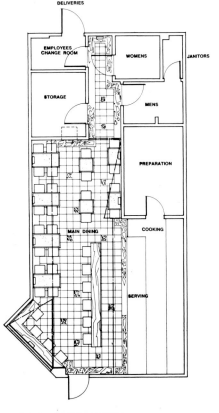

HUNTER'S HAMBURGERS

Marina Del Rey, CA

The 30-seat restaurant takes up only 1175 sq. ft. in a new shopping plaza in the Marina Del Rey area of Los Angeles and according to the designer, Gina Muzingo, "it is heavy on visual stimulation."

"There's neon on the outside of the building that I wanted to bring inside" — and she did it. Neon seems to zig-zag, wave, slash and thunderbolt through the interior — up and below the metal grid that separates the black ceiling and the silvery ducts snaking around from the textured, paint splattered panels and the swirling sheets of metal sculpture that form a fascia over the glass block service counter. In addition to the "visually exciting" neons, the designer has included halogen lights in warm blue wall sconces and downlights concealed in the soffit to provide some "traditional" illumination. The incandescent fixtures that are surface mounted in this jumping, jiving place are there "more as pieces of art than as functional lighting devices." Very little is "normal" or "traditional" here except maybe the oak wood and red accented stools, tables and dining counter.

Design: Muzingo Associates, Los Angeles, CA
Principal: Gina Muzingo
Photographer: Peter Malinowski

MACHEESMO MOUSE

Portland, OR

The client loves the off-beat and the unusual and that allowed the architects/designers to have fun with the architecture. Though each store is still "site specific," there is a common sharing of concepts, colors and materials that reinforces the award-winning look of Macheesmo Mouse, a local fast-food chain with a Mexican accent that boasts of great burritos. In the 23rd Ave. location, entry is gained through a separate structure, encased in diamond plate, set at an angle to the facade. Garage doors open in fair weather to blur the distinction between inside and outside.

The interior is "bright and brash." "Materials commonly encountered in the American landscape have been utilized in sometimes uncomfortable juxtapositions; laminates to corrugated sheet metal, diamond plate to glass — all to create tension and energy." Corrugated metal-faced counters, folding chairs, dropped brightly colored ceiling grids, boldly checkerboarded floors, neon signage and bold, bold graphics are combined with witty and irreverent architectural touches to make this not "a place of refuge from the often chaotic world, but an extension of it." The daring owner, Mr. Warren, describes his hip, healthful Mexican fast food place as a "bus station of intergalactic vehicles."

Design: Vallaster and Corl, Architects, Portland, OR
Photographer: Rick Rappaport

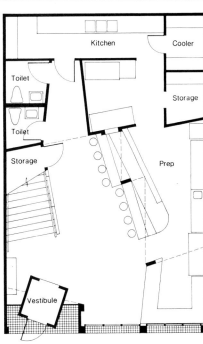

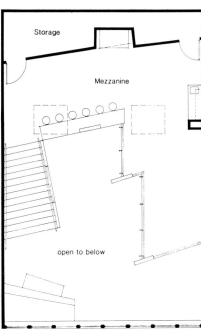

TACO BELL

Winston-Salem, NC

This nationwide fast food chain also serves up Mexican-style foods and it is quite different in look from Macheesmo Mouse. Oriented to families and more often to suburban locations, the Taco Bell restaurants are usually spotted off the road or highway by the southwestern stuccoed facade, the arched windows and the terra cotta tiled mansard roof. Inside the spaces are bright, cheerful and ready to receive all. In the new prototype the floors are covered with a pale gray tile while walls, counters and dividing partitions are veneered with white tiles accented with red, green and black tiles. The service counter is reached by means of a route outlined by red enameled railings and the kitchen with its stainless steel equipment and white tiled walls is on view for all to see. Red and green neon ribbons wind around the stepped surfaces that lead up to the dropped acoustic tile ceiling. The red, white and green scheme is repeated on the laminated table tops. The chairs are enameled in gray with cherry red upholstery. The usual free standing unit is from 2500 to 30,000 sq. ft. while shopping center pads are often limited to 5000 sq. ft.

BEEFHANS

Bahia Center, Acapulco, Mexico

Located on the lower level and reaching up to a second level of the bright new shopping mall on the very busy main street in

Acapulco is this exciting, high-tech fast food operation designed to entice and please both the local shoppers and the international travelers who find their way here. It is eye-filling and offers a variety of tempting and satisfying snacks all prepared in full view of the diners. There is a bakery that turns out hot muffins and pastries, the scent of which fills the soaring space, while burgers and fries sizzle and sputter on visible grids or fryers. In a refrigerated, glass-enclosed butcher shop hang choice cuts of meat.

In the center of the lower level is a condiment station color-filled with decorative accessories. The black and white strong floor pattern is complemented by the terra cotta enameled beams, columns and walls and everywhere the neon signage and graphics add a delightful shimmer to the fun and fresh interior. Diners are invited to sit on a raised level — or further up on the mezzanine under the trussed ceiling.

Photographer: Father & Suns

167

FLAMINGO BAY

New York, NY

The clients, Susan and Leonard Fox, wanted a flamingo theme for their hot dog/tropic drink stand and that is what Evelyn Sherwood and her partner Heinrich Spillmann gave them. The brilliant red flamingo flaps its wings on the illuminated facade of the corner shop, and hot pink plastic ones parade up and down inside of the 440 sq. ft. space — all on view through the eight foot high windows set into a turquoise grid. Two six foot bifold windows, on one side, can be opened when the weather is fine and promising. The interior sparkles with color and the neon signage is perched along with the flamingos on the green grass shack roof that is the soffit over the service counter. On that back counter sits four drink tanks, three juice spray dispensers, a soda tower and coffee machine. For the "brilliance and color rendering" desired, Ms. Sherwood selected a lighting plan that combines fluorescents with quartz halogen fixtures. From the multicolored tiled floor to the Memphis patterned laminate counter to the squiggles of color running around columns and walls, — the lighting plan succeeds.

Design: Evelyn Sherwood Designs, Inc., NY
Architect: David Turner, Arch.
Photographer: Frank Zimmerman

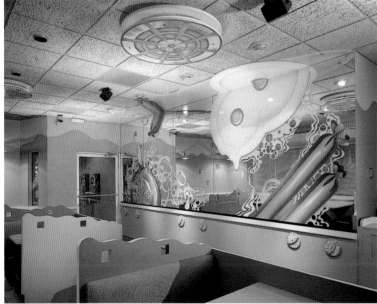

BYRON'S HOT DOG STAND

Clybourn, Chicago, IL

"We wanted to put some fun and fantasy into a fast food atmosphere," says Charles Rizzo, principal at Skyline. The 1700 sq. ft. space is divided into a dining area of 100 seats and a service counter section. An undulating counter, veneered in white and aqua does the separation and backed up to the eating counter are wavy panels of turquoise, edged in white, that in turn separate one booth from the next. Upholstered back rests are attached to the laminated panels which are "cheese-holed" with square cut outs.

The "grill" is actually a 20' mirrored wall with "grease stains" sandblasted onto the surface. Giant, colorful cut-outs of frankfurters, french fries, onion rings and eggs fried sunny side up are applied onto the mirror and even over onto the ceiling. Flying space station lighting fixtures float on the ceiling. On the pale gray laminated wall under the mirror/grill are knobs for the kids to play with — to turn the heat up on what's cooking.

Design: Skyline Designs, Chicago, IL
Photographer: Tim Wilson

169

CHICK*FIL*A

Prototype Store

Chick-Fil-A is one of the largest privately held restaurant chains and the fourth largest chicken chain in the country. By the end of 1990 there were almost 450 units including mall operations as well as free-standing restaurants.

Based on interviews with hundreds of customers and mall shoppers, the concept for the newly redesigned spaces came into being. According to the management of Chick-Fil-A, — "The customers had a major impact on the design. They helped conceptualize, define and refine a mall restaurant look that would be the best in the industry."

The architects/designers new updated interior design includes a more comfortable seating arrangement, softer lighting, new product photography and a counter designed for better service. Mall and free standing space both are schemed in red, white and natural woods accented with touches of brass. Many service areas and counters are faced with tiles and red enameled lamp shades hang over them and pour flattering incandescent light onto the freshly prepared foods. Greenery complements the warm color scheme.

Along with the new contemporary accents are the khaki and maroon uniforms designed to coordinate with the interiors. On page 170 is a free standing shop and on page 171 is one of the newer mall units.

Design: Babcock & Schmidt, Bath, OH

PIZZA CONNECTION

Independence Mall, Kingston, MA

The Pizza Connection is a pizza/bar located in a food court where its design creates a "futuristic and dominant image" with a sharp contrast of color that is sure to attract customers' attention. The conventional bulkhead is set back to create a niche for dispensing the pizza. Four giant triangular red and black banded torcheres highlight the logo and the yellow menu board under the yellow soffit that carries the stainless steel and red neon signage. The color scheme of black, red and yellow with stainless steel under the ceiling of pinpoint lights is very effective.

Design: Tony Chi/Albert Chen, NY

MADE IN JAPAN

Toronto, Ont.

Another food operation popular in Canada — and spreading is Made in Japan which presents "good healthy nutritious foods prepared fresh" before the diner. Here, too, stands range between 375 and 500 sq. ft. and the design is simple, contemporary but suggests a Japanese heritage. The grid and shoji screen motif appear throughout; the counter is made of a red lacquered metal grid framing transluscent panels that allow the light behind to come through. The black grid overhead carries the neon signage. Like Mrs. Vanelli's the red and black plastic laminates are used with the white tiled working interior and the foods are prepared under fluorescents but presented under incandescents.

MRS. VANELLI'S PIZZA & ITALIAN FOOD

Toronto, Ont.

These mall units, mostly in Canada, range in size from 350 to 500 sq. ft. and they depend upon the food courts for seating. The counter joins red and black laminates with illuminated glass blocks while, above, a silvery metal grid supports the logo and signage in red and white neon. The interior of the stand is lined with white ceramic tiles accented with the red and black laminates and the stainless steel pizza oven is in full view. The overhead lighting mixes fluorescents over the work area with recessed high hats over the food presentation. The menu board is black and red and highlighted by rear illumination.

PICKLE PEPPER & ROMAINE

San Francisco, CA

The client, Tony Keng, wanted a prototype design for a chain of "fast food health restaurants that could convey the snap and crispness" of its vegetarian name. The designer focused on the area the customers could see and came up with a plan that was based on clean lines — and stayed within the tight budget. To economize, Calvin Lau relied on sparsely colored mosaic floors and counters, colorful neon signs and sharp red enameled downlights. To keep the small space open and airy and yet take advantage of the exposed natural brick wall and the very high ceiling, — the other walls were painted white and the counter tops were also finished in white. Acoustical tile ceilings, anodized aluminum framing and plastic laminates also helped to keep the design within the budget.

The menu board on the white wall is outlined with white neon and the yogurt toppings on the white counter are contained in inexpensive, off-the-shelf, red plastic dishes. The fresh fruits for juice are also neatly contained in plastic fronted cannisters under the menu board and just over the juicer.

Almost white on white, the prototype has been cloned and more Pickle Pepper & Romaine health-fast-food shops should be cropping up in the San Francisco area.

Design: Calvin Lau Designs, San Francisco, CA
Photographer: Michael C. Lewis

174

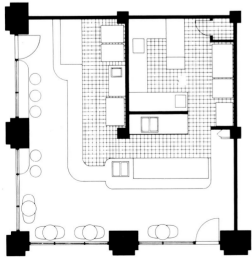

LE CROISSANT

New York, NY

In just a few years Le Croissant has evolved from a bakery/cafe into a growing chain of more than 20 units offering breakfast, lunch and snack alternatives to Metropolitan N.Y. customers. Not only do the outlets feature the croissants in their name, but there are filled croissants, puff pastries, danishes, soups, salads, breads and a variety of muffins. The French-style cafes vary in size from 300 to 2500 sq. ft. and usually provide some seating for the diners. Blue is the color of Le Croissant. "Studies have shown that blue relaxes patrons which is the effect we're trying to create," says Gary Goddard, director of design and construction. "Blue takes Le Croissant out of the realm of fast food restaurants that feature 'hurry-up' color schemes of red and orange and separates them from the hamburger shops down the street." Often classical music is piped in and wicker baskets hold the displayed baked goods. Fresh flowers on the counter and green plants on walls and hanging from ceilings add a friendly, at-home quality to these shops that tend to slow down the "fast" in their foods.

Design: Gary Goddard, V.P. Le Croissant
Photographer: Father & Suns

AU BON PAIN

Copley Plaza, Boston, MA

Au Bon Pain is another bit of Paris brought to the American Public. These foodservice bakeries are located in malls as well as in downtown areas, and they are "in the business of providing a light breakfast, and a light lunch in an urban setting with an emphasis on fast food, a quality product and a friendly welcome."

The average store is about 1500 sq. ft. with seating for about 100. Customers are routed in with bank-style railings and the counter people at the white and chrome counters take orders and money. Another crew makes up the orders and hands them out at the end of the counter — or may bring them to the customer at the table. Red, white and gray, plus shots of black is the usual color scheme for an Au Bon Pain and the back lit photographs add color and sparkle to the warmly lit interiors. White table tops with red lacquered bentwood chairs are signature elements in the store design.

Design: Todd Lee Associates, Boston, MA
Photographer: Steve Rosenthat, Auburndale, MA
Harvard Square, Cambridge, MA
Photographer: Jean Smith, Cambridge, MA

JACKETS

New York, NY

Since the menu specializes in stuffed potato skins — what the British call jackets — Samuel Arlen and Frederick Fox turned the space into a giant potato skin. "The patrons become the conceptual 'filling' for the baked potato and the earthly colors of the plastic laminated walls and wood floor support the conceit."

The "crumbling walls" represent the torn off top of the baked potato as well as "the top of a building with tornado sheared walls — roof gone and open to the sky — a few structural members of the black grid form remain."

Design: Arlen/Fox, Architects, NY
Photographer: James D'Addio

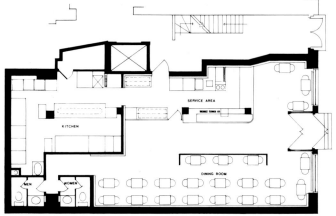

SEAPORT FRIES

South St. Seaport, New York, NY

The color scheme selected for Seaport Fries which is located next to and shares the kitchen equipment with South Philly Steak & Fries is wood that has been stained yellow and a deep forest green — set off by brightly backlit ribbed glass tiles. The materials and colors were chosen to "complement the warm and satisfying food and to counteract fries 'junk food' image." The stainless steel equipment is in sight behind the serving counter and up front — a tumbled mound of scrubbed potatoes stars under the row of piercing low voltage, tungsten lamps. To unite the two fast food concessions a checkered band of tiles, at eye level, sweeps across both spaces and a diamond motif appears in the front of the counters.

Design: Evelyn Sherwood Designs, NY
Photographer: Frank Zimmerman

TURKEY, TURKEY

Willowbrook Mall, Wayne, NJ

"We used white and light gray tile with blue accents to achieve a crisp, clean look — with a touch of pumpkin to warm it up. The jumping back-lit blue glass tiles add life and energy." To complete the overall image a turkey, outlined in neon, has a "kicking neon leg" that makes him appear to be dancing. The grill is front and center and the roasting ovens are directly behind to emphasize the freshly cooked concept.

Design: Evelyn Sherwood Designs, NY
Photographer: Frank Zimmerman

1 POTATO 2

New Hope, MN

Nothing small potatoes here! The company has been a leader and specialist in bringing healthy potato treats to the public in many states of the Union. The compact setting has white ceramic tiled walls on the interior banded and highlighted with metallic bronze-brown tiles that are also the background for the signage fascia above that carries the white neon logo. The face of the counter is paved with large squares of white faience tiles. Brass drop lights hang over the counter top and brass strips outline the glass sneeze guards in front of the prepared foods. Black accents and back lit photo-murals on the menu board contribute to the look of 1 Potato 2.

KERNELS WORLD

Potomac Mills, Prince William, VA

This Canadian company is moving down into the States with their many flavors of popcorn. The quick-snack is displayed in an almost totally yellow ambience to accentuate the golden color of the corn. Yellow tiled walls are further energized with back lit photographic panels and the yellow plastic laminated counter features a large variety of flavors, mixtures and gift items in the wide and deep glassed space. A row of white cannisters with incandescent spots highlights the encased products with warm light.

Design: Scott Staiman, Pres. of Kernels

MINTERS

World Finance Center, New York, NY

Located in the 5-story atrium of the super elegant Winter Garden at the World Finance Center is Minters, a tropical bar and gourmet fast food eatery. The free standing kiosk, complete with circular trellis work serves espresso/cappuccino as well as cocktails — after five. One of the four circular torcheres with concealed turquoise neon is set atop the 8' high trellis supported by four ash columns

Inside, gourmet snacks and pastries are served from display counters ornamented with unique architectural metal cutouts. Some of the elements playfully suggest ice cream cone sprinkles — and these "sprinkles" also appear — like confetti — in a floor

to ceiling mural in the space. The remaining walls are glazed "to add depth and illusion." Precast terrazzo tiles of different colors are laid in geometric patterns on the floor outlined with alternating jade and yellow tiles. The same motifs and colors are used throughout as a graphic design "signature." A 1½" diameter rod painted bright red projects from the ceiling and curves through the space. It carries 20 mini MR16 lamps that plug into the ceiling with curly black cords. The blue lens Dana light that is used at the edge of the circular trellis "creates a visual presence for Minters but does not put them in competition with the surrounding brass canopies of the atrium" or with the cool, marble refinement of Ceasar Pellis overall Atrium design.

Design: Tony Chi/Albert Chen, Architects, NY
Photographer: Dub Rogers, W.H. Rogers III, NY

EVERYTHING YOGURT / BANANAS

Gateway Center, Newark, NJ / Summit Mall, Akron, OH

A crossword puzzle was selected as a decorative motif for the 1200 sq. ft. Gateway Center store since it is one that commuters relate to — and most of the traffic here is made up of commuters going to and coming from NY. "In addition to playing off the commuter customer base, the graphic quality of the crossword puzzle made it an effective theme, says Mark Dranfield, Dir. of Design for Everything Yogurt. "We are able to incorporate the concept into our storefront signage and mural, as well as integrate it into the rest of the interior by using a striking black and white grid."

The attractive white interior is spiked with bands and blocks of black plus rose/pink and yellow tiles set into the white tiled walls and counters. The pink picks up the Everything Yogurt logo and the yellow is the Bananas part of the joint operation. An acid green complements them both.

In a traditional mall situation, as at the Summit Mall, the two entities are adjacent to each other and the neon signage and the different color schemes serve to separate them from each other yet they do colorfully contrast — and therefore — complement each other.

Design: Mark A. Dransfield, Director of Design & Construction
Photographer: Bill Higgins

BEN & JERRY'S

Waterbury, VT

Ben & Jerry's "Vermont's finest all-natural Ice Cream" started up only 13 or so years ago in a renovated gas station in Burlington, VT. They soon gained a following anxious to try their "funky, chunky flavors" and in only three years were hailed by *Time* magazine as "the best in the world."

The company owned and franchised operations (about 100) are usually spotted by the popular spotted black and white cows grazing on a billiard green field under an aqua sky with fluffy white clouds. The motif appears outside (as in the Santa Monica location next to Frank Gehry's Museum of Art complex on Main St.) and inside over the white tiled counters. The Ben & Jerry's logo, in red, black and pink, appears in continuous bands over the counters and around the undecorated walls. Simple white bistro chairs and tables serve as seating for those who don't want the ice cream to melt.

Ben & Jerry's sponsors a foundation which awards monies to non profit and charitable organizations and it supports projects "which are models for social change — which enhance peoples' quality of life."

GEORGIE PORGIE

Westport, CT

This super-smart, 3000 sq. ft. Ice Cream Parlor/Gift Shop is located in super upscaled Westport and it is all pretty, pink and polished metal. The ceiling is pink gridded with shiny chrome bands and stepped down waves of pink plastic laminates connect the ceiling to the wall behind the gleaming counter. Some walls are sheathed in vertically striped metal laminates — like bans of corrugated metal running from floor to ceiling. The chairs and tables that can accommodate 67 customers are pink enamel and laminates edged in chrome and they are fixed into the pink and black patterned tile floor. The designer opted for a look that was part high-tech and part '50s — but in pink since it is "a color that represents sweets." The slickness of the materials provide the high-tech look that Kaye was after.

Pink neon ribbons and a continuous band of complexion bulbs outlines the semi-circular candy and gift counter up front which is also faced with the corrugated material. Shiny black complements the silver tones and accentuates the blushing pinks. Throughout the space recessed incandescents add to the flushed and flattering light of Georgie Porgie.

Design: Designs by Kaye, Westport, CT
Principal: Arnold Kaye

HAAGEN DAZS SOFT

Walden Gallery Mall, Buffalo, NY

Haagen Dazs Soft was designed as a prototype to introduce the new "soft" product. "Many of the materials were selected as metaphors for the soft ice cream including the corrugated metal for the counter fronts, the stainless steel, the curved steel shapes on the back counter and the curved glass display case." The all important toppings are angled — slanted so that even the children can see all the offerings. The decorated cones are presented below — also set at a child's eye level. To reflect a "sense of quality" and softness, curved white marble tops and

other areas of marble were included in the design. Back lit photographs make an important impact on the otherwise low-lit burgundy colored menu board. A few red neon accents sparkle the classy stand while still projecting "an energetic and fun image." "We tried to present the product's distinctive image through quality materials and clean graphics which you don't always find in fast food shops," says Martin Dorf, architect/designer.

Design: Martin Dorf Associates, NY
Graphic Designer: Craig Carl, NY

189

HUMPHREY YOGURT

Brentwood Gardens, Brentwood, CA

Pink, white and pretty — and a cheerful setting to "appeal to the upscale clientele of the sophisticated retail complex." In addition to the blended yogurt treats there is a cafe menu of light sandwiches, and pastas as well as espresso and frappe drinks. Lots of natural daylight streams in and bounces off the light colored walls and the pale, soft gray tiled floors and several droplights highlight the up front service/cashier station. For extra general illumination the acoustic tiled ceiling is interrupted with baffled fluorescent fixtures. Recessed spots light up the rear working space and the pink laminated counters and cabinets.

Design: Muzingo Associates, Los Angeles, CA
Photographer: Peter Malinowski

YOGEN FRUZ

North York City Centre, Toronto, Ont.

The facade of this 175 sq. ft. shop is not finished like the typical "ice cream or yogurt shop"; it is faced with Italian black granite which sets flush the rainbow of neon streamers that are inset into the counter. The neon is covered with smoke finished plexiglass. Light blue Corian surfaces the counter top and the canopy overhead repeats the black form with neon ribbon stripes along with the store's signage superimposed. The menu boards are custom made with back lit presentation photographs. "The store was designed to be uniquely high tech and attractive — reflective of our product and our fast paced customers."

Design: Martin Hirschberg Design Associates, Toronto, Ont.

TCBY

Prototype Store

With almost 2000 stores in all 50 states and in 5 foreign countries, TCBY is recognized as one of the major leaders in the frozen yogurt field. This shop is rich in natural wood textures used with assorted white ones; white ceramic tiled floors, white brick faced walls, textured walls and ceiling. Light oak tables and chairs are joined by a counter that simulates an outdoor stand with cedar shingled roof and a chocolate brown laminate front to contrast with all the whites and lots of green plants seem to thrive in the mostly fluorescent illuminated store. In addition to the frozen yogurt machines behind the "shack" there is a take-out freezer with prepackaged products.

CALIFORNIA COOL

Eaton's, Montreal, Canada

The facade on the aisle is a giant checkerboard design of blue and cream colored ceramic squares with mirrored panels flanking either side of the entrance into the shop. The customer moves in under the illuminated aqua blue and California peach/pink sign fascia — all very Southern California — into a brightly lit space of pastel peach tiles on the walls and a curving counter accented with black/white checkered border and an aqua menu board on the back wall. Glass cases, almost down to the floor, present the products under the spots lined up in the dropped ceiling over the counter.

Design: International Design Group, Toronto, Ont.

FRESHENS YOGURT

Prototype Store

The award winning design with the Freshens name called for a "clean, fresh and natural image" and thus much of the space is surfaced with "clean looking" white ceramic tiles and laminates. The real design splash was reserved for the sign bulkhead area. An extensive overhead truss system supports a combination acrylic and neon sign which resembles the Freshen's logo. "Our visual surrounding or perception created by the truss attracts mall shoppers from afar." Once at the counter, it is the display of the toppings, the interior graphics, menu board and the merchandised clear acrylic display containers that take over.

Design: KB Design Group, Pittman, NJ
Principals: Jerry Keller/Ben Bonaccorso
Photographer: Beth Singer, Franklin, MI

BRESLER'S ICE CREAM & YOGURT

Des Plaines, IL

Bresler's Ice Cream is a national franchise company with shops in more than 30 states that feature also frozen yogurt and baked goods for dessert. The sharp facade consists of light oak wood pilasters holding up a grid of oak that crosses over the entrance into the shop and it is brilliantly accented with red and white tiles in an haphazard pattern that backs up the company name. The counter stretches from the mall aisle to the rear of the space and it is faced with slats of oak bordered with the tomato red laminate. In some of the Bresler operations the splash area behind the work counter is covered with red tiles and an awning of shiny red fabric serves to hide the lighting over the display and service counters. The awnings carry the product identification. The warm lighting enhances the homey and friendly attitude of the Bresler operation.

BOOMERANG

Santa Monica, CA

Main St. in Santa Monica is having a renaissance. In addition to the much discussed Frank Gehry Museum of Art complex, stylish clothing and furniture stores — and restaurants have appeared on the street. Boomerang is a charming ice cream/yogurt/baked goods oasis on the street with a few tables inside but chairs are lined up outside under the sheltering awning where patrons can lick, savor, slurp and swallow while watching the passing parade. White tiled floors and wainscotted walls are accented with dubonnet and green. The serving counter as well as the coffee and baked goods station adjacent are faced with honey oak veneers as is the railing in front. The dropped ceiling over the counter carries the recessed lights while daylight filters in through the large plate glass window up front. The green band that encircles the square space is the green of the awning on the street.

Design: Carol & Gary McNamara, owners
Photographer: Father & Suns

JENNY'S

Philadelphia, PA

Jenny's is located near South St. in Philadelphia which is an area known for its unique environment, eclectic clientele, thriving retail market and active night life. In the midst of this stir of excitement the 1500 sq. ft. space serves up ice cream and desserts in an ambience that is suited to its neighborhood. The facade is mostly glass blocks contained in a framework of stainless steel with neon signage over the wide expanse of clear glass that opens up the store. Inside the floors are tiled in white, counters are covered with white laminates and the walls recede in a deep slate blue. The stools that line up along the counter that runs along the wall opposite the serving counter are painted hot pink and upholstered in ice-cream-parlor pink. Glass cases show off the products and neon graphics generate the excitement in the low-lit interior.

Design: SRK Architects, Philadelphia, PA

T.J. CINNAMONS

Kansas City, MO

T.J. Cinnamons calls itself "the home of the original gourmet cinnamon rolls" and the smells that drift out from the white, brown and beige shops equipped with ovens where the cinnamon rolls are freshly baked, make the shopper believe that claim. The preparation of the deliciously sticky rolls is part of the draw and behind the glass partitioned area (right) the rolls are prepared all through the day. The walls and floors are white and the counters are horizontally banded in cinnamon, cafe au lait and cream — in keeping with the menu. The curving glass fronted case puts row after row of tempting morsels on display and black pendant shades direct the warm light onto the baked goods. Cinnamon brown laminated tables are teamed with natural bent wood chairs upholstered in black — the accent color in the warm, neutral scheme. The menu board is also black framed in oak. The soffit is decorated with bands of brown and black and the T.J. Cinnamon logo is decoratively applied.

CINNABON

Seattle, WA

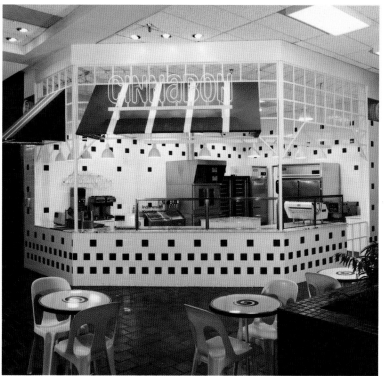

Another readily recognized name in malls and also associated by smell as well as sight is Cinnabon. These shops are "positioned as a bakery and not as a fast-food restaurant or food stand" though they are often located in food courts where the hot and sticky product is usually consumed quickly — on the spot.

Italian cremo marble counter tops, stainless steel and white ceramic tile with cobalt blue accents are usually found in Cinnabon shops. "The visual effect is that of a crisp, clean, modern facility with traditional overtones of the old neighborhood corner bakery." In addition to the cinnamon rolls assorted drinks are served and the coffee is especially blended for these bakeries. Usually molded white plastic chairs and round tables with the Cinnabon logo swirl are provided for the shoppers.

A cobalt blue striped with white awning identifies the shiny white tile and marble shop below and the Cinnabon logo appears on the awning. Below the awning, on the white framework support, a row of white metal lamp shades serve to illuminate the up front work area and service counter.

FOOD COURTS

Food courts are here to stay and in those malls where they were not a part of the original planning they are definitely important elements in the renovations and expansions of those malls and centers.

Food courts are focal points in malls. They are places people meet and gather, replenish and rest and get ready for another go around. The "New Age Food Court" not only offers "cuisine entertainment" it is often as much a destination or draw as the anchor store. It is the place people come to be — to eat — to meet — to rest. It is here that the mall designer/architect can let loose — let his/her imagination soar — fly up, float and fill the space with plantings, fountains, banners and graphics under what is often a glass vaulted or multi-mullioned skylight roof. Just as the mall designer can make a strong statement about the mall with the imagery he/she brings into the food court, the individual vendors and concessions are often invited to make creative and attractive statements too about themselves; who they are and what they have to offer. And — more and more — that expression is made through visual merchandising and display with the food preparation up front under the bright lights and the neon signs.

Food courts and the dining areas are no longer being tucked away in far off corners or hidden down in the lower depths. They are being brought out into prominent areas and are often the center or core around which the retail shops of the mall seem to orbit. They are given architectural importance and filled with gracious amenities; benches, flowering plants and exotic trees — steps, platforms, mezzanines and levels from which to delight in the panoramic views of fountains, waterfalls, or silent pools filled with pennies and dreams. There may be antique merry-go-rounds to amuse the children and entertain the old — bandstands or stages for concerts and performances and staged fashion shows presenting the garments and merchandise available from the retailers in the mall. This is the world of entertainment; it is where food, drink and fun come together and you really don't have to buy anything to be part of the action.

But, how can you not buy a cup of freshly brewed coffee — or some cookies at Mrs. Field's or Original Cookie — or some sticky buns at Cinnabon or T.J. Cinnamons when the wonderful aromas of the freshly baked cakes, cookies and buns fill the garden-like setting — and all around you people are eating with such relish? Seen through the trees and shrubs and protected under a canopy of canvas or an overhang from the floor above is the sparkle and glitter of neon signs, blinking lights, bright colors. The shaded-from-the-daylight area is usually filled with the food concessions and in that semi-darkness the richness of color and light enhances the products being offered.

A food court can have as few as six to eight food merchants but what is very important is the mix and variety of the foods being offered. Regional malls that range from 750,000 to one million square feet may have as many as eight to 12 food concessions though some developers, like Rouse, will opt for larger food courts with up to 15 stands. The larger malls — over one million square feet — may have even more concessions. Always it is getting the right mix that counts and the right mix for one mall may be the wrong one for another. Fashions in food, like in clothes, are ever changing and from the examples we presented in our chapter on Fast Foods — the mainstays of the food courts — the possibilities are stunning. Is Japanese "in"? Is Mexican "out"? What's hot and what's cooling off — is it Ice Cream or is it Yogurt — fresh fruits for toppings or Thai for trying? Is this a location where "fat and cholesterol" are a problem or do the customers even think of them when it is time for snacking? The variety and mixture is out there and the right ones are the ones the customers will be attracted to and that will complement the other foods being offered.

Food Courts are "in" and here are some visual examples of why they are so important today.

Myrtle Square Mall

RIVERWALK

New Orleans, LA

The Rouse Co. development features a high tech, bright and animated food court where food concessions are lined up one next to the other along the brick tiled walkway under the high, corrugated metal ceiling filled with trusswork, service pipes and big fat caterpillars that are the air venting system. Suspended down from above are three dimensional, gold leafed symbols of the various foods available at the stands tucked back under the dropped ceiling on the right. Canvas streamers serve as decorative dividers between the graphic "signs." On the left beyond the natural wood, stand-up, communal dining tables is the sit down area. This is set up for those who want to relax while dining under rows of white lamp shaded incandescents suspended from the enveloping white trusswork.

Architect: Perez Associates
Project Designer: Communication Arts Inc., Boulder, CO
Developer: Rouse & Co.
Photographer: R. Greg Hursley, Inc.

THE ARCADE-CHAMPLAIN MALL

Brossard, Que.

This food court can seat approximately 450 persons and it was recently expanded in keeping with the still growing mall. A peaked glass and metal roof divides the food court while it also fills it with daylight. The structural beams and girders are painted deep red to go with the tubular arches and "gazebos" that punctuate the sitting area. The floors are paved in a medley of assorted colored granites accented with patterns and bands of ceramic tiles. The supporting columns and enclosing partitions are finished in pale gray with tile bordered decorations. Lots of plants and trees are landscaped throughout the food court adding verdant splotches to the neutral gray and red area. The food stands are lined up along the two long walls with a continuous awning-like framework of dark gray metal frames filled with glass. Dark gray lampshades extend out and down from that angled fascia.

Design: Gervais-Harding & Assoc. Design, Inc., Montreal, Que.
Architect: Shaprio & Wolfe, Architects, Montreal, Que.
Developer: Ivanhoe, Montreal, Que.
Photographer: Andre Doyon

SHAWNEE MALL

Shawnee, OK

The sitting area for this mall is landscaped like an outdoor garden. The light wire metal chairs are set out on gray, white and black ceramic tiled floors that also suggest the traffic patterns. The tables are clustered around dark gray slate covered wells filled with green trees and with flowering plants. Old fashioned white globe street lamps add more to the ambience than the light they produce since the glass and metal framework ceiling really turns the space into an open-to-the-sunlight setting. Surrounding the seating area, flashes of colored neons beckon to the food concessions.

Architect: Omniplan, Dallas, TX
Developer: Marathon, U.S. Realties
Photographer: James F. Wilson, Dallas, TX

THE GARDENS

This sparkling and effervescent addition to the mall scene on Florida's east coast is upscaled and polished. The food court is located on the second level around the giant multi-angled atrium courtyard with its white beamed and trussed glass skylight. The white supporting columns that carry the weight of the floating metal lace structure are rooted in planter boxes that are filled with lush green foliage. There are raised dining areas as well as those flush with the encircling food concessions and restaurants. Several tables are highlighted with white canvas umbrellas. Pressed glass droplights provide the illumination where and when the sunlight doesn't do it.

Architect: James P. Ryan, Assoc.
Photographer: Father & Suns

FIRST CANADIAN PLACE FOOD COURT

Toronto, Ont.

Located on the second level in a prominent metropolitan high rise/office complex, the food court seemed to be an "invisible component." Not only did the architects design a "presence" for the food court, — they replanned the public circulation, rezoned the concessions for maximum exposure and maximized the seating capacity all in keeping with existing basebuilding materials. The result, shown here, is an exciting, upscaled dining atmosphere in sophisticated black and white, marble and lacquered surfaces. The very low ceiling was turned into a floating design with pink neon tubes washing the ceiling. Dramatic uplights join the recessed ceiling downlights to create the ambient lighting.

Design: Camdi International
Project Manager: Patty Xenos

CARREFOUR ANGRIGNON

Montreal, Que., Canada

The task the designers faced here was to create a food court in the 250 store shopping center that would be a destination in itself. The immense greenhouse architectural construction controlled the atmosphere and while it enhances the illusion of space — it "distorts the sense of scale and intimacy normally associated with shopping" and dining. It was necessary to create a real attraction to the center of the court — to make the concession shop fronts visible from there. The fountain in the heart of the court surrounded by the graceful rotunda accomplished that. It also provided a sense of scale and furthered the garden image. Garden chairs and oversized lamp posts balance the scale and suggest a Continental ambience. Planters and parasols link the outdoors with the indoors and a circular ring above the fountain houses a series of theatrical spotlights that create a dramatic, theater-like atmosphere once the daylight has gone.

The concession facades are designed within a light metal framework that gives the illusion of a series of linked together kiosks.

Design: Camdi International, Montreal, Que.
Project Manager: Patty Xenos

WESTWOOD MALL

Houston, TX

The food court is sprawled out over acres of quarry tile under a superstructure of glass held in a web of white metal rods and beams and as the focal point — an old fashioned carousel. Juxta-posing the wonderful old merry go round rich in gilt carvings, strutting steeds and polychromed panels — all outlined in dots of light is a sleek, sharp, sophisticated contemporary design executed in shiny black in a field of white. From rods that stretch across the space hang assorted canvas streamer/banners and plants and trees sprout up between the tables set out under the daylight. Escalators carry the shoppers down to this expansive dining area surrounded by food concessions set beneath the overhanging mezzanine.

Developer: Marathon U.S. Realties
Photographer: James F. Wilson, Dallas, TX

206

ALEXANDRIA MALL

Alexandria, LA

What is good in Texas also seems to be just fine in Louisiana and here, too, the carousel takes center stage under the wide open glassed-in atrium. The 50,000 sq. ft. food court can accommodate up to 550 persons between the wood floored central area and the tables and chairs in the more garden-like setting on the white quarry tile level with the stone lined fountains and planters filled with greenery. To further the outdoor, garden setting trees seem to be growing up out of the wood covered floor. The two level, hand painted Italian carousel sparkles with light bulbs but the neon signs around the open space accented with metal grid units call the shoppers to the food concessions visible through the trees. Quartz lamps attached to the floating grids light up the courtyard along with the uplights on the columns.

Architect: Food Court: Wudtke, Watson, Davis & Engstrom,
San Francisco, CA
Mall: Architecture Plus, Montroe, LA
Developer: Marathon H.S. Realties
Photographer: James F. Wilson, Dallas, TX

A&S PLAZA

New York, NY

A 1200 seat food court, The Taste of the Town, graces the vertical shopping mall in midtown NYC. Sixteen international and
American eateries surround the large dining court and the giant
gazebo, outlined in white bulbs, forms the central focal point for
the space. The vaulted blue ceiling above it is filled with the illusion of floating clouds. The floors are paved and patterned with
gray and white marbles while black, white and gray ceramic tiles
are freely applied throughout the designed area. The backlit
glass block enclosures follow the sweep of the hemi-spherical
dome construction of the gazebo and plants in planters bring the
outdoors into this very indoor and ultra urban space.

Architects: RTKL Associates, Baltimore, MD
Developer: Melvin Simon Assoc.

THE FASHION MALL

Plantation, FL

The Fashion Mall "combines the color and imagery of the Caribbean with forms and materials of 19th century exposition buildings." The central court serves as a "village square." Upscale tenants fill the mall and upscaled shoppers find their way to the food court located in the atrium — under the six story high glass dome that floats over the palm trees and semi-tropic plantings — the Mediterranean inspired tile patterns. The friendly and pleasant eating environment also draws office workers, hotel guests and residents from nearby.

Design: RTKL Associates, Baltimore, MD
Photograph: Scott McDonald, Hedrich/Blessing

KILLEEN MALL

Killeen, TX

This 660,000 sq. ft. regional mall boasts an 8776 sq. ft. food court that can seat almost 350 persons. Deep green lacquered columns line up as the long axis of the food court under a series of skylights, laid out in echelon, break up the ceiling. White tiles pave the dining area and the area is bordered with natural terra cotta colored "bricks." Oak planters, dividers and bow back chairs add a traditional, folksy touch while the blue, green and red neon stripes that encircle the columns and zigzag through the space — following the pattern of the skylights — supply the fun spirit to the court.

Architect: Clyde M. Wess
Developer: Marathon U.S. Realties
Photographer: James F. Wilson, Dallas, TX

PECANLAND MALL

Monroe, LA

Almost one quarter of the nearly one million sq. ft. regional mall is set aside for the food court, the 16 concessions, the 485 seats and the two sit-down restaurants. The wide and spacious food court takes on a fairyland quality with trees aglitter with white bee-lights and graceful white metal arches swinging back and forth over the dining areas — also outlined in white bulbs. The peaked skylight fills the fountain and foliage enhanced space with light during the daylight hours but at night the space is touched with magic and the metal grids and spanning arcs turn this into a special place to be.

Architect: Architecture Plus, Monroe, LA
Developer: Marathon U.S. Realties
Photographer: James F. Wilson, Dallas, TX

PARK PLAZA MALL

Little Rock, AR

The food court takes up 11,500 sq. ft. on the lowest level of the mall and the 400 + seats are set out in the center of the light filled atrium. The ten food concessions are set back under the walkway of the first level and the shine and glow of the neon signage and the individual stands' lighting get a full play in the semi darkness that surrounds the atrium.

Architect: Architecture Plus, Monroe, LA
Developer: Marathon U.S. Realties
Photographer: James F. Wilson, Dallas, TX

FOOD COURT

Caribbean Beach Resort, Orlando, FL

A food court NOT in a shopping center! Here is a rather unique one located in the fifth largest resort in the country and it was thematically designed to resemble five Caribbean villages each reflective of a particular island's culture and character. All the villages and features in the 200 acre resort of over 2000 rooms are grouped around a 32 acre lake. The Old Port Royale is the focal point of the lakefront with a Customs House where guests register and the food court that is reminiscent of an old-world village with costumes, props and interior design to suit.

Inspired by old San Juan, the space is designed to look "as if it

has evolved over many years" and inside a half dozen food concessions provide food for the 500 patrons who can be seated here. It is a special boon for families who are "doing" Disney World who want fast food — fast service — at fair prices for their families — in a fun setting. Even though it isn't formal dining, there is lots of atmosphere, theater and visual delights for the diners to partake of, along with the food in this out-of-the-past, romantic environment.

Architects: Fugleberg Koch Architects, WinterPark, FL
Interior Design: Wilson & Assoc.
Photographers: Erin O'Boyle, Melbourne
Robert Miller, Dallas, TX

UNION STATION FOOD COURT

Indianapolis, IN

The 70,000 sq. ft. food court was a primary design focus in the conversion of the 100 year old historical station of one of the Nation's oldest lines into a retail environment. The space had to have an overall identity while still providing individual identities to the vendors and the dining areas. A stairwell connects the second level food court with the main retail level and it is highlighted with the new "track side" logo on a large colorful neon sign. Eighteen food tenants are lined along one side of the court with 12 retail shops and four-in-line restaurants on the opposite side. Neutral piers delineate each space though each store front has its own fresh facade treatment and brightly colored

awning. A palette of 33 colors was used on store awnings, banners, signage, railings and ceiling mechanical and structural supports.

A graphic version of a 40 foot train dining car with 20 booths provides additional seating for the food court. The familiar R.R. clock got new colored details and it is in full view of the shoppers and dinners in the court.

Design: T.L. Horton Design, Inc., Dallas, TX
Principal: Tony L. Horton
Developer: Moor & South
Photographer: Joe Akers/Akers Photography

THE SHOPS AT TABOR COURT

Denver, CO

Architect: Urban Design Corp.
Project Designer: Communication Arts, Inc., Boulder, CO

COLLISEUM

Hampton, VA

Like its name — it has an almost classic quality; a rotunda surrounded by post modern rather than corinthian columns — supporting a sky-blue dome pierced with recessed spots and floods. The floor is laid in a grid pattern of white granite squares set with black diamonds and a square-in-a-square of tiles is laid in the center of the rotunda. From here the shopper enters onto a long aisle with a peaked roof cooly illuminated by hidden fluorescents. The black and white scheme and the patterned use of the tiles reappears, with variations, to face the assorted concession counters along the aisle. More round columns balanced on black cube bases continue on the thoroughfare to support the triangular structures that interrupt and define the ceiling construction.

Architect: RTKL Associates, Baltimore, MD
Developer: Mall Properties Inc., NY

PACIFIC PLACE

Westlake Center, Seattle, WA

Graphic design takes over to explain and enhance the architecure. Under the lowered ceiling the food concessions are set up in a sawtooth plan under an open canopy of deep red metal rods which frame the individual concessions and their neon signage. The same rich deep red appears on the tiled fronts of several of the serving counters and on the dining tables with the molded gray chairs. Between the glow of neons and the reflected warmth off the red surfaces hit by the recessed incandescent lamps in the ceiling the area is comfortable and intimate compared to the main sitting area beyond. The main seating is out under the atrium opening and amidst the swirl of neon graphics that outline and highlight the court's signage.

Architects: RTKL Associates, Baltimore, MD
Project Designers: Communication Arts, Inc., Boulder, CO
Photographer: R. Greg Hursley

FORD CITY

Chicago, IL

Inside the court — it's hot! It sizzles! The area is suffused with red and pink light which is flattering, fun, stimulating and exciting — and it also guarantees a quick turn over of seats. The ceiling consists of a series of raised rings outlined with frames that extend below the common ceiling line. Hidden fluorescents flush the raised areas while recessed lamps in and around the ringed frames send warm light down onto the tables below. Torcheres, growing out of partitions and dividers, send up light to illuminate the Food Court signs. Exotic palms grow in the planters set around the dining area — in the equally exotic ambience.

Architect: Loebl Schlossman Hackl, Assoc.
Project Designers: Communication Arts, Boulder, CO
Photographer: R. Greg Hursley

NORTHCROSS MALL

Austin, TX

The renovated mall now has a crisp, contemporary look for the '90s since the architectural designers upgraded all aspects of the design from lighting to landscaping to signage to flooring and a new exterior facade. The goal was to strengthen the mall's image as "the premiere family oriented entertainment mall in the region." Of course, the food court got special attention. Terra cotta and beige accented with teal was used throughout the mall but in the food court the red neon accents causes the area to blush. The 20,000 sq. ft. court has 12 food concessions and it is located next to the Olympic size skating rink. The 400 seats are raised up on a mezzanine so that the diners can watch the skaters just below. Colorful neon signs identify the food concessions while brilliant banners and quartz lighting adds to the glow.

Design: Hambrecht Terrell International, NY

EAST HILLS MALL

Bakersfield, CA

To create a patio-like atmosphere the design accent is on "cool and comfortable" and the color palette consists of aqua, blue, mauve and lots of white and neutral gray along with plenty of plants and ficus trees. Overhead, off the white metal beams and trusses of the expansive skylights, hang canvas banners that add bright accents to the cool color sheme. Floors and dividing partitions in the dining area are faced with ceramic tiles that echo the above color scheme and the canvas umbrellas over the light looking blue enameled chairs and tables do the same. Off the supporting columns are decorative white globe lights that provide general illumination at night.

Developer: Hahn Co.
Photographer: Sandra Williams

FOX HILLS MALL

Culver City, Los Angeles, CA

The new food court "Food Fare on Three" is readily identified by the blue metal grid that acts as a backdrop for the neon sign and mall logo. Inside the food court the same blue metal, grids span across the ceiling dividing it into sections and spaces. Neon is used extensively for signage around the perimeter walls where the food concessions are located. The neon adds to the contemporary image favored by the trendy W. Los Angeles patrons who come to Fox Hills Mall.

Developer: Hahn Co.
Photographer: Fernando Escovar

PICNIC PLACE

Fashion Place, Murray, UT

Picnic Place is a new addition to the center and it features two eating areas. First is the enclosed glass garden patio where shoppers may relax and enjoy a light repast while watching the outdoor activity. The second area is located in the 450 seat food court where the elevated platform with seating is surrounded by greenery and small fountains. The polychrome graphic banners add a sense of excitement to the airy space conceived in black, white and gray — and mainly surfaced in tiles.

Developer: Hahn Co.

INDEX